KV-512-547

The Stage and Screen Quiz Book

By the same author:
The Questionmaster's Quizbook
The Seventies Quizbook
The Sixties Quizbook
The Twentieth Century Quizbook

The Stage and Screen Quizbook

Compiled and introduced by
David Self

Thorsons
An Imprint of HarperCollins*Publishers*

For
David 'Hitch'

Thorsons
An Imprint of HarperCollins*Publishers*
77–85 Fulham Palace Road,
Hammersmith, London W6 8JB
1160 Battery Street,
San Francisco, California 94111–1213

Published by Thorsons 1994
1 3 5 7 9 10 8 6 4 2

© David Self 1994

David Self asserts the moral right to
be identified as the author of this work

A catalogue record for this book
is available from the British Library

ISBN 0 7225 2971 6

Printed in Great Britain by
HarperCollinsManufacturing, Glasgow

All rights reserved. No part of this publication may be
reproduced, stored in a retrieval system, or transmitted,
in any form or by any means, electronic, mechanical,
photocopying, recording or otherwise, without the prior
permission of the publishers.

Contents

Introduction

There's no business like show business. As Ava Gardner put it, 'It's the kissiest business in the world. You *have* to keep kissing people.' That is certainly how 'luvvies' (as actors have sometimes been labelled) can appear to those on the edge of their world.

But almost every one of us remains fascinated by the stars of the theatre, cinema, radio and television–and they inevitably try to live up to our expectations or at least to follow the advice of the film mogul Cecil B. De Mille: 'Remember you are a star. Never go across the alley–even to dump garbage–unless you are dressed to the teeth!'

The questions in this book are about that world of entertainment–from the ballet to old-time music hall; from Shakespeare to television 'soap operas' and from the first silent films to the cinema's latest blockbuster. Many of the questions are about the shows we love (or hate) and talk about each day. Some of the more difficult ones should tax the serious film buff and the most dedicated theatre-goer!

The idea for the book came from a radio quiz I invented and developed with David Hitchinson, a drama producer in BBC World Service. For 15 years, I had been writing general knowledge questions for a variety of radio and television quiz shows–and also writing the series of quizbooks of which this is one of the latest (books that include *The Questionmaster's Quizbook* and *The Sixties* and *Seventies Quizbooks*). Then (in 1991) David asked me to help him develop a new radio quiz that tested actors on their knowledge of theatre, films and musicals. The result was the show we called *Break A Leg*.

It's rather strange title comes from the fact that it is considered bad luck in the theatre to wish anyone good luck. Consequently, when actors want to wish each other good luck (especially just before a 'First Night'), they say 'Break a leg!' That is, they wish each other bad luck in the hope of cheating fate! In Germany, incidentally, they go even further and wish each other 'Hals und

Beinbruch' (literally, a neck-and-leg fracture).

David and I did have some worries that *Break A Leg* might appeal only to those who liked and knew about the theatre. But from all the comments we received from right around the world, it was much appreciated and thoroughly enjoyed by people from very different backgrounds. It even made front-page news in the *Buenos Aires Herald*!

So, like the radio show, this book is not just for 'luvvies' and their friends. Its 2,500-plus questions are for everyone who enjoys watching television or videos, listening to the radio and/or going to the theatre or the cinema.

All the questions have been thoroughly researched–and it is hoped that questionmasters can rely on the answers supplied! Once again I must express my real gratitude to Monica Dorrington for her considerable help in word-processing and checking the text of the book.

I hope this book will help everyone running quizzes in clubs, village halls and pubs–and in hospitals and schools, the services and in the social sections of large firms. Amateur dramatic societies will find it provides a basis for many enjoyable evenings, either for members' private amusement or for more public battles, perhaps against rival societies. Most of all, however, I hope it generates many hours of entertainment for family showbiz addicts–either as a 'run-your-own-quiz' guide or as a 'keep-the-family-happy-in-the-back-of-the-car' book!

This is in fact a book of quizzes for all occasions and for when you just want to test your own knowledge.

You will find the answers on the page following each quiz. This means that you can refer to them easily if you are the questionmaster of a 'public' or 'semi-public' quiz, and you can also avoid any temptation to cheat if you are testing yourself! There is space on each page which you can use either for filling in the answers or for keeping the scores–and if you do this lightly in pencil, you can use the book for this again and again. The answers to three quizzes (Numbers 33, 66 and 99) are at the back of the book–simply because the questions for these rounds take up two pages.

These three quizzes and several others in the book (e.g. the 12 'Hidden Titles' rounds) were originally devised for *Break A Leg*. When these quizzes are being used in contests between two teams, one team could 'perform' the passages or dialogues to the other team (and, of course, to any audience). The 'Hidden Titles' dialogues are under copyright but may be used in amateur quizzes, provided that their source is acknowledged.

Likewise, the clues in the five 'Get the Guest' rounds may be spoken by members of one team to test the opposing team. Four points could be awarded if the guessing team 'gets the guest' after just one clue; three points after two clues; and so on. The same rules could apply to other quizzes with the same format, such as Quiz No. 97 (The Number One Tour) and No. 105 (International Theatre).

In many of the 'standard' rounds, there are 24 questions per quiz (plus a tie-breaker) arranged in two groups of 12–so the quizzes are suitable for two teams (Team A and Team B), of three, four or six contestants each.

• The questions are graded within each game–a pair of 'matched', easier ones for the first team-member, then getting progressively harder.

• The questionmaster can select from the questions in each round depending on the number of team-members and the degree of difficulty required.

• Phonetic pronunciations of certain words likely to trip up a quizmaster are given; and, as well as the required answer, 'acceptable' variants are also included to eliminate argument and reinforce the questionmaster's authority!

• Tie-breaker questions vary from the light-hearted to the trivial, and from the moderately testing to the fiendishly difficult.

• The questions appear on the right-hand pages, with the solutions (and the tie-breaker) on the following (left-hand) page–with the exception of rounds 33, 66 and 99, mentioned above.

• In short, the intention is to provide quiz organizers with 120 quizzes ready for use 'straight from the book' without further sorting, checking, verifying, etc.

• All the questions relate to the world of the performing arts–from 'straight' theatre to 'showbiz'.

In serious or public competitions, it is always wise to formulate the rules quite precisely and to publish these rules in advance of the competition.

A basic decision facing any quiz organizer is whether each question is 'open' to the first competitor who can offer an answer or whether questions will be posed to contestants (or teams) in turn. The advantage of the first style is that it generates much more pace and excitement. For it to function efficiently, each individual contestant (or, in the case of team quizzes, each team) should have a buzzer or light which will indicate quite clearly who was first to offer an answer. In this type of quiz, a person should be required to answer as soon as he buzzes, otherwise he merely handicaps his opponents.

Those organizing the more formal type of quiz may like to know of an electronic device which gives a professional touch to any quiz and makes the life of the quizmaster very much easier. The Jaser Quizmaster has been designed for use in team quizzes and consists of a small console for the quizmaster and two lamp units. Each of these units consists of four push-buttons and lamps and allows individual contestants to press their team's buzzer and to light up an adjacent lamp. As soon as one person presses a buzzer, all the others are disconnected and so there can be no argument as to who has buzzed first! For further details of the equipment contact: Jaser Electronics Limited, 1 Castle Mews, Rugby, Warwickshire, CV21 2XL.

Of course quizzes may be organized in which questions are posed to contestants in turn and then there is no need for any bells, buzzers or lights! Such quizzes may not generate so much pace but they do provide a longer period of entertainment. They also allow each contestant to participate equally rather than favouring the fastest thinkers. This format may be more suitable when contestants are of different ages—but even here you can bring in a timing element or impose time-limits for individual questions or sequences of questions. You can also add variety by letting your teams confer in some rounds but not in others.

How you score is again up to you. You may want to award two points for a correct answer, one point for a 'half-correct' answer, one point for a corrected answer from the opposing team if a question is passed over, and nothing for a wrong answer. Or you may like to give a sequence of, say, six questions to one team (or person), and then to award a bonus if that team or person gets them all right.

In most quizzes an unanswered question or one answered incorrectly is usually offered to the opposing team or to the other individual contestants. Because they have had longer to think and possibly because their recollection has been helped by the previous attempt, the question will normally be easier for them than it was for the first team to answer. It may therefore be decided not to award as many points for answering someone else's question or for answering second as for answering your own question or for answering first.

In any quiz, the quizmaster needs to be able to decide immediately whether he or she can accept a particular answer or not. For this reason, questions must be unambiguous and phrased so as to elicit brief and concise answers which are clearly either right or wrong and not matters for debate. It is hoped that the questions in this book will satisfy these demands and will therefore be helpful in running quizzes that are not interrupted by delays, arguments or confusion!

You should not therefore need an adjudicator, because the questions are deliberately straightforward, the answers short and to the point, and any alternative answers are supplied: but you may need a scorer, or at least someone to check the quizmaster's scoring!

The quizmaster should always make it clear whether he or she has accepted an answer or not. From an audience's point of view, it is also more interesting if they can see the score and not rely on the scorer's announcement at the end of each round. A simple scoreboard can be made in the style of the old-fashioned cricket scoreboard where the score was shown by numbers hung on nails.

And finally, you can make up other kinds of rounds to go with the quizzes here. You can show slides, posters or newspaper cuttings—for example of stars or recent or current shows; you can play brief excerpts from recordings, or a pianist can play snatches of tunes from musicals; you can invent questions about current radio and television series and the latest cinema and video releases, or about local performers. If you look closely at the questions in this book you will have not only the material for 120 ready-made quizzes but also the ideas for many, many more.

So what else is there to say except–Orchestra! Lights! Ring up the curtain and let's do the show right now. And, as they say in the business, 'Break a leg!'

No. 1 Beginners, Please

An introductory round of general questions about the theatre.

a1 In a song, who was advised not to put her daughter on the stage?

b1 *Who would receive training at RADA–and for what does it stand?*

a2 In the theatre, what are the 'flies'?

b2 *And what is an 'aside'?*

a3 In the theatre, what is an 'angel'?

b3 *And what is an 'ad lib'?*

a4 What is or was vaudeville?

b4 *What colour costume is usually worn by a pierrot?*

a5 Who wrote and made famous the song 'Stop Yer Ticklin' Jock'?

b5 *Which music hall star sang 'I'm one of the ruins Cromwell knocked about a bit'?*

a6 The Olivier, the Lyttleton and the Cottesloe are all part of which building?

b6 *Where is the Royal Shakespeare Company's London home?*

a7 Which comedian in one of his guises used the phrase 'Oo, you are awful, but I like you'?

b7 *Which comedian was famous for raising his glasses and saying 'There's no answer to that'?*

a8 In the London theatre, which is the longest-running play ever?

b8 *Which bird is also the name of a play by Chekhov?*

a9 What nationality was the playwright Strindberg?

b9 *From which island did the actress Lillie Langtry come?*

a10 What is the name of R. C. Sherriff's famous play about the First World War?

b10 *Arthur Miller's play* The Crucible *deals with witchcraft in which American town?*

a11 In which language did Aristophanes write his plays?

b11 *What nationality was the playwright Henrik Ibsen?*

a12 By what names are Dr Evadne and Dame Hilda better known?

b12 *Which pop star has played Jesus in* Godspell, *Ché Guevara and Lord Byron?*

No. 1 Answers

a1 Mrs Worthington (by Noël Coward)
b1 *Actors/actresses; Royal Academy of Dramatic Art*
a2 The tower above the stage (where scenery can be hoisted, etc.)
b2 *A remark addressed to the audience and not to the other characters on stage*
a3 A backer; someone who puts money into a play
b3 *A line not in the script, an improvised line*
a4 Light entertainment (sequence of songs and sketches; originally French music hall)
b4 *White (with black pompoms)*
a5 Sir Harry Lauder
b5 *Marie Lloyd*
a6 Royal National Theatre (accept: the National Theatre or just 'the National')
b6 *The Barbican*
a7 Dick Emery
b7 *Eric Morecambe*
a8 *The Mousetrap*
b8 The Seagull
a9 Swedish
b9 *Jersey (she was known as 'The Jersey Lily')*
a10 *Journey's End*
b10 *Salem*
a11 Ancient Greek (accept: Greek)
b11 *Norwegian*
a12 Hinge and Bracket
b12 *David Essex*

Tie-breaker

Q How many actresses were there in Shakespeare's theatre company?
A *None (all the parts were played by men and boys)*

No. 2 Hidden Titles–1

Within each of these dialogues are hidden the titles of a number of musical shows. Can you spot the titles and say who wrote each group of musicals?

Team A

Mother So Romeo, what is thy news?

Romeo Mother, me and Juliet, we want to get married.

Mother There must be a proper wedding. We must organize it properly. Bells, flowers, the sound of music.

Romeo No, at once. We want to get married at once. Allegro.

Mother That's just a pipe dream. The king and I have decided. When–

Romeo We'll elope. Go far away. To the south Pacific. Or somewhere out west. America. The state of Oklahoma!

Mother You're making me dizzy. It's like being on a carousel.

Romeo (*As he goes*) Oh what a beautiful morning. I'm in love, I'm in love...

Team B

(*He is enthusiastic, excited; she is just a little world-weary*)

He Darling, I'm going to buy you a little present.

She You never know what to get me.

He Leave it to me. It'll be out of this world.

She So long as it's not silk stockings. I mean, let's face it, I've got hundreds. I'd like something to go with my little black dress.

He Anything goes with a little black dress. Oh, and I'm also going to get something for the boys.

She What can...can you be thinking of?

He Just a little something to celebrate. I mean, theirs was such a gay divorce.

No. 2 Answers

Team A titles
Me and Juliet
The Sound of Music
Allegro
Pipe Dream
The King and I
South Pacific
Oklahoma!
Carousel
all by Richard Rodgers and Oscar Hammerstein II

Team B titles
You Never Know
Leave It to Me
Out of This World
Silk Stockings
Let's Face It!
Anything Goes
Something for the Boys
Can Can
The Gay Divorce (NB Although the film version was called *The Gay Divorcée*, the original stage show was *The Gay Divorce*)
all by Cole Porter

No. 3 Vision On

An introductory round of general questions about television.

a1 In a soap opera, which famous character was played by Jean Alexander?

b1 *And which character was played by Doris Speed?*

a2 In which soap have we met Matt and Dolly Skilbeck?

b2 *In which soap were Bobby and Sheila Grant leading characters?*

a3 For which role was Jack Warner best known?

b3 *Which series has featured policemen called Carver, 'Tosh' and Monroe?*

a4 In the Fifties, in which 'club' did Andy Stewart and Jimmy Macgregor sing?

b4 *Who was the 'stupid boy' in Dad's Army?*

a5 In *Upstairs, Downstairs*, who played the butler, Hudson?

b5 *And in* The Professionals, *whom did the same actor play?*

a6 Which star used to start his shows by shouting 'Wakey Wakey'?

b6 *Figgis, Glover and Norman were characters in which comedy series?*

a7 Who played Rigsby and Norman Tripper?

b7 *Which television comedian was famous for playing a blood donor?*

a8 Which actor played Shelley?

b8 *In* Last of the Summer Wine, *what part is played by Kathy Staff?*

a9 On television, who became famous for his Madhouse?

b9 *In which television hotel did a waiter come from 'Bar–th–elona'?*

a10 Which actor played the television detective, Columbo?

b10 *And which actor played Ironside?*

a11 Who played Starsky in *Starsky and Hutch*?

b11 *Who played Sergeant Bilko?*

a12 Of which television series were Nerys Hughes and Elizabeth Estensen the stars?

b12 *In which comedy series did we meet Father Duddleswell?*

No. 3 Answers

a1 Hilda Ogden (*Coronation Street*)
b1 *Annie Walker*
a2 *Emmerdale Farm*
b2 Brookside
a3 Dixon (of Dock Green) (PC George Dixon)
b3 The Bill
a4 *The White Heather Club*
b4 *Private Pike, played by Ian Lavender ('Stupid boy' was Captain Mainwaring's regular dismissal of the hapless Pike)*
a5 Gordon Jackson
b5 (George) Cowley
a6 Billy Cotton
b6 Only When I Laugh
a7 Leonard Rossiter
b7 *Tony Hancock*
a8 Hywel Bennett
b8 *Nora Batty*
a9 Russ Abbot
b9 Fawlty Towers (*Manuel, played by Andrew Sachs*)
a10 Peter Falk
b10 *Raymond Burr*
a11 Paul Michael Glaser
b11 *Phil Silvers*
a12 *The Liver Birds*
b12 Bless Me, Father

Tie-breaker

Q What product was featured in the first commercial shown on ITV?
A *Gibbs SR Toothpaste (accept: toothpaste)*

No. 4 Curtain Up!

a1 As what did Grimaldi achieve fame?

b1 And for what is Marcel Marceau famous?

a2 Which Australian housewife (and 'megastar') is associated with Barry Humphries?

b2 Which former governor of California was once a film star?

a3 Which London theatre boasted during the Second World War that 'We never close'?

b3 Who wrote the long-running play The Mousetrap?

a4 Which dramatist wrote the play *The School for Scandal* ?

b4 And who wrote The Doctor's Dilemma?

a5 As what did Isadora Duncan achieve fame?

b5 And as what did Jenny Lind achieve fame?

a6 Who wrote the Aldwych Farces *Rookery Nook* and *A Cuckoo in the Nest* ?

b6 And who wrote the play French Without Tears?

a7 In which art has Joan Sutherland achieved fame?

b7 For what kind of entertainment did Vesta Tilley become famous?

a8 Who wrote the plays *Roots* and *I'm Talking About Jerusalem*?

b8 And who wrote Brief Encounter?

a9 Who was the first actor to be made a Lord?

b9 Which French actor sang 'Louise' and starred in Gigi?

a10 In medieval times, what were performed in the streets of Chester, York and Wakefield?

b10 Who is the central character who is murdered in the play Murder in the Cathedral?

a11 In the play *Pygmalion*, who was Eliza Doolittle's teacher?

b11 On which children's book is A. A. Milne's play Toad of Toad Hall *based?*

a12 Which director founded Theatre Workshop, first in Manchester and later at Stratford East?

b12 Which Anglo-Irish director was the first director of the Stratford, Ontario Festival?

No. 4 Answers

a1 A clown (in pantomime)
b1 Mime
a2 Dame Edna Everage
b2 Ronald Reagan
a3 The Windmill
b3 Agatha Christie
a4 Sheridan (Richard Brinsley)
b4 G. B. Shaw
a5 A dancer
b5 A singer ('The Swedish Nightingale')
a6 Ben Travers
b6 Terence Rattigan
a7 Opera (accept singing)
b7 Music hall (singer)
a8 Arnold Wesker
b8 Noël Coward
a9 Lord Olivier (Sir Laurence, 'Larry')
b9 Maurice Chevalier
a10 Mystery or miracle plays; plays that re-told stories from the Bible
b10 Thomas à Becket (Becket of Canterbury)
a11 Professor Henry Higgins
b11 The Wind in the Willows (by Kenneth Grahame)
a12 Joan Littlewood
b12 Sir Tyrone Guthrie

Tie-breaker

Q In 1960, the first theatre to be opened in the City of London for 300 years was created by Bernard Miles. What is the name of the theatre?
A *The Mermaid*

No. 5 Get the Guest–1

How many clues do you need before you can identify each of the following film personalities? (See page **9**)

Guest A
1 I was born in Massachusetts, USA and studied acting in New York.
2 Directors didn't think I was beautiful enough for romantic roles–but that didn't stop me winning Oscars in 1935 and 1938.
3 I often, but not always, played cruel and selfish characters–as, for example, in the film *All About Eve*.
4 In a much later film, I terrorized my screen sister and audiences–who worried about Baby Jane.

Guest B
1 When I was a boy, I borrowed my father's ciné camera to film toy trains.
2 By the age of 21, I was directing television series–including *Columbo*.
3 My first cinema hit broke all box office records.
4 I've made a 'purplish' story about racial conflict, and had a number of close encounters–as well as losing an ark.

Guest C
1 My parents, Mr and Mrs Gumm, managed a theatre in Lancaster, California where I first sang in public.
2 My four marriages all ended in divorce.
3 My daughter also became a star of film, stage and cabaret.
4 My biggest hit came when I was just 16 and only just setting out along the yellow brick road.

Guest D
1 I was born in Miami, USA, in 1927 but grew up in the Bahamas.
2 I took acting lessons at the American Negro Theater in New York and this training led to roles on stage and in films.
3 In 1963, I won an Oscar for the film *Lilies of the Field* but by then I'd already been in *The Blackboard Jungle*.
4 In my best-known film, I was a New York cop, solving a murder in the heat of a small town in the southern USA.

No. 5 Answers

Guest A
Bette Davis (1908–1989)
After studying at the John Murray Anderson School, she made her Broadway bow in *Broken Dishes* (1929). She won the Best Actress Oscar for *Dangerous* (1935) and a second Best Actress Oscar for *Jezebel* (1938). She was memorable as the flamboyant but vulnerable theatrical 'grande dame' Margot Channing in *All About Eve* (1950) and the grotesquely deranged Jane in *Whatever Happened to Baby Jane?* (1962).

Guest B
Steven Spielberg (1947–)
The hit in clue 3 is *Jaws* (1975); the film about racial conflict is *The Color Purple* (1985). His other films include *Close Encounters of the Third Kind* (1977), *Raiders of the Lost Ark* (1981), *ET–The Extra-Terrestrial* (1982), *Back to the Future* (1985) and its two sequels, *An American Tail* (1986), *Who Framed Roger Rabbit?* (1988), *Arachnophobia* (1990), *Jurassic Park* (1993) and Schindler's List(1993).

Guest C
Judy Garland (1922–1969)
She made her stage début at the age of three and performed as a member of The Gumm Sisters, making her film début with them in *The Meglin Kiddie Revue* (1929). She signed a contract with MGM that brought her employment in the studios' musicals and as Dorothy in *The Wizard of Oz* (1939) and won a special Oscar for her performance of the song 'Over the Rainbow'. Her daughter was Liza Minnelli, who starred in the film *Cabaret* (1972).

Guest D
Sidney Poitier (1927–)
Raised in the Bahamas, Poitier started his acting career as a member of the American Negro Theater. He was especially notable as a student in *The Blackboard Jungle* (1955). He won an Oscar for his performance as a handyman in *Lilies of the Field* (1963) and was soon established as the cinema's first black superstar. His best-known film is probably *In the Heat of the Night* (1967), co-starring Rod Steiger.

No. 6 First Reel

An introductory round of general questions about the cinema.

a1 What was the name of Gene Autry's horse?

b1 *And what was the name of the Lone Ranger's horse?*

a2 Who played an American president in *Dr Strangelove*?

b2 *Who played Rudolf Rassendyll in the 1937 version of* The Prisoner of Zenda*?*

a3 Which film featured the Irving Berlin songs 'Easter Parade' and 'White Christmas'?

b3 *In the film* Singin' in the Rain, *which star was singing in the rain?*

a4 Name one of Bing Crosby's two co-stars in the 'Road' films.

b4 *Who co-starred with Celia Johnson in the film* Brief Encounter*?*

a5 In which film did Baloo sing about the bare necessities of life?

b5 *By what name is Bruce Wayne of Gotham City better known?*

a6 About which ship, principally, is the film *A Night to Remember*?

b6 *Over which river did prisoners build a bridge in a film starring Alec Guinness?*

a7 Which British film told the story of Eric Liddell and Harold Abrahams?

b7 *Who played eight roles in the film* Kind Hearts and Coronets*?*

a8 Which young star became a teen idol with his film *Rebel Without a Cause*, released after his death in a car crash?

b8 *Which was the Beatles' first film?*

a9 · Which former film actress married Prince Rainier of Monaco?

b9 *Which film star visited Hanoi to show her disapproval of America's role in the Vietnam War?*

a10 Who co-starred with Meryl Streep in the film *The French Lieutenant's Woman*?

b10 *Which film star was married to Lauran Bacall and won an Oscar for his role in* The African Queen*?*

a11 About what activity was the film *Pumping Iron*?

b11 *Which film, set in the future, is all about a violent game played on roller-skates?*

No. 6 Answers

a1 Champion
b1 *Silver*
a2 Peter Sellers
b2 *Ronald Colman*
a3 *Holiday Inn*
b3 *Gene Kelly*
a4 Bob Hope or Dorothy Lamour
b4 *Trevor Howard*
a5 *The Jungle Book*
b5 *Batman*
a6 The Titanic
b6 *The River Kwai*
a7 *Chariots of Fire*
b7 *Sir Alec Guinness*
a8 James Dean
b8 A Hard Day's Night
a9 Grace Kelly
b9 *Jane Fonda*
a10 Jeremy Irons
b10 *Humphrey Bogart*
a11 Body-building
b11 *Rollerball*

Tie-breaker

Q Name the seven dwarfs in *Snow White*
A *Bashful, Doc, Dopey, Grumpy, Happy, Sleepy and Sneezy*

No. 7 Songs from the Shows–1

In which musical does each of the following numbers occur:

a1 'Oh What a Beautiful Morning'?
b1 *'Sixteen Going on Seventeen'?*
a2 'I Feel Pretty'?
b2 *'Doin' What Comes Naturally'?*
a3 'I'm Gonna Wash that Man Right Outa My Hair'?
b3 *'I'm Getting Married in the Morning'?*
a4 'Tomorrow'?
b4 *'Thank Heaven For Little Girls'?*
a5 'If I Were a Rich Man'?
b5 *'Ol' Man River'?*
a6 'Vilia' and 'Girls, Girls, Girls'?
b6 *'The Drinking Song' and 'To the Inn We're Marching'?*
a7 'The Worst Pies in London'?
b7 *'Hare Krishna'?*
a8 'It Ain't Necessarily So'?
b8 *'Fascinating Rhythm'?*
a9 'You're Getting to Be a Habit with Me'?
b9 *'You'll Never Walk Alone'?*
a10 'Who Wants to Be a Millionaire'?
b10 *'Sit Down, You're Rockin' the Boat'?*
a11 'Macavity'?
b11 *'Brush Up Your Shakespeare'?*
a12 'Willkommen'?
b12 *'I'll See You Again'?*

No. 7 Answers

a1   *Oklahoma!*
b1   The Sound of Music
a2   *West Side Story*
b2   Annie Get Your Gun
a3   *South Pacific*
b3   My Fair Lady
a4   *Annie*
b4   Gigi
a5   *Fiddler on the Roof*
b5   Showboat
a6   *The Merry Widow*
b6   The Student Prince
a7   *Sweeney Todd–The Demon Barber of Fleet Street*
b7   Hair
a8   *Porgy and Bess*
b8   Lady, Be Good!
a9   *42nd Street*
b9   Carousel
a10   *High Society*
b10   Guys and Dolls
a11   *Cats*
b11   Kiss Me, Kate
a12   *Cabaret*
b12   Bitter Sweet

Tie-breaker

Q   From which rock opera come the songs 'It's a Boy', 'Cousin Kevin' and 'Pinball Wizard'?

A   Tommy

No. 8 Introduced By...

Who is remembered as the main (or only) presenter of these television series?

a1   *Blind Date?*

b1   The Generation Game*?*

a2   *Mastermind?*

b2   That's Life*?*

a3   *The South Bank Show?*

b3   Juke Box Jury *(as originally seen on BBC TV)?*

a4   *Take Your Pick?*

b4   Opportunity Knocks*?*

a5   *The World of Sport?*

b5   It's A Knockout*?*

a6   *University Challenge?*

b6   Sale of the Century *(when seen on ITV)?*

a7   *Mr and Mrs?*

b7   The Good Old Days*?*

a8   *What's My Line* (when seen on BBC TV)?

b8   *The original* Tonight *programme (on BBC TV)?*

a9   *Nationwide?*

b9   Monitor*?*

a10   *Ask the Family?*

b10   Come Dancing *(from 1957–1972)?*

a11   *The Sky At Night?*

b11   *The original* Face to Face *interviews?*

a12   *Civilisation?*

b12   Life On Earth*?*

No. 8 Answers

a1   Cilla Black
b1   *Bruce Forsyth (also Larry Grayson)*
a2   Magnus Magnusson
b2   *Esther Rantzen*
a3   Melvyn Bragg
b3   *David Jacobs*
a4   Michael Miles
b4   *Hughie Green*
a5   Dickie Davies
b5   *Stuart Hall (originally David Vine) (assisted by Eddie Waring)*
a6   Bamber Gascoigne
b6   *Nicholas Parsons*
a7   Derek Batey
b7   *Leonard Sachs*
a8   Eamonn Andrews
b8   *Cliff Michelmore*
a9   Michael Barrett (also Sue Lawley)
b9   *Huw Wheldon*
a10   Robert Robinson
b10   *Peter West*
a11   Patrick Moore
b11   *John Freeman*
a12   Kenneth Clark (Lord Clark)
b12   *David Attenborough*

Tie-breaker

Q Which announcer introduced programmes on the first night of BBC Television in 1936 and on ITV on its first night in 1955?

A *Leslie Mitchell*

No. 9 The Big Screen

a1   In the film *Live and Let Die*, who played Bond?

b1   Who played the title role in Spartacus?

a2   In the film *Genevieve*, what was Genevieve?

b2   And what was the 'Titfield Thunderbolt'?

a3   Which famous British film company is associated with the symbol of a man striking a gong?

b3   Which famous Hollywood film company uses a mountain peak surrounded by a circle of stars as its trademark?

a4   With what emblem do MGM films begin?

b4   Which film company's emblem is a shield bearing the company's initials?

a5   Which handsome male star appeared in *The Color of Money*, *Cocktail* and *Days of Thunder*?

b5   And who was a cyborg killer in The Terminator?

a6   Who wore drag in *Some Like It Hot*?

b6   In Goldfinger, what was the name of the villain with the dangerous hat?

a7   Which American child film star became the US representative to the United Nations in 1969?

b7   Which Swedish film actress became a Hollywood legend and starred in such films as Mata Hari, Grand Hotel and Queen Christina?

a8   In the film *Oliver*, what role was played by Ron Moody?

b8   And who played Dr Doolittle on screen?

a9   In which film did Bing Crosby first sing 'White Christmas'?

b9   In which film did Judy Garland sing 'Over the Rainbow'?

a10   Which rock star appeared in the films *Ned Kelly* and *Performance*?

b10   Which pop singer starred in the films The Man Who Fell to Earth and Merry Christmas, Mr Lawrence?

a11   Who created the Muppets?

b11   Which of Disney's films was an attempt to interpret classical music?

a12   For what sort of films was John Grierson famous?

b12   Which political leader were Leni Riefenstahl's pre-war films meant to glorify?

No. 9 Answers

a1 Roger Moore
b1 *Kirk Douglas*
a2 A veteran car (1904 Darracq)
b2 *A very old branch line railway train*
a3 The Rank Organisation
b3 *Paramount*
a4 A (roaring) lion
b4 *Warner Brothers*
a5 Tom Cruise
b5 *Arnold Schwarzenegger*
a6 Tony Curtis and Jack Lemmon
b6 *Odd Job*
a7 Shirley Temple (married name: Shirley Temple Black)
b7 *Greta Garbo*
a8 Fagin
b8 *Rex Harrison*
a9 *Holiday Inn*
b9 The Wizard of Oz
a10 Mick Jagger
b10 *David Bowie*
a11 Jim Henson
b11 Fantasia
a12 Documentaries
b12 *Hitler*

Tie-breaker

Q Can you name the five Marx Brothers?
A *Chico, Harpo, Groucho, Zeppo (who left the act after five films) and Gummo (who left the act very early on)*

No. 10 Where's That From?–1

These quotations come from plays, films and shows–but which ones?

a1   'Frankly my dear, I don't give a damn.'

b1   *'Elliptical billiard balls.'*

a2   'Come up and see me sometime.'

b2   *'I never travel without my diary. One should always have something sensational to read in the train.'*

a3   'What do we want with eggs and ham
When we've got plum and apple jam?
Form fours, right turn,
How shall we spend the money we earn?'

b3   *'You ain't heard nothing yet.'*

a4   'My name is Corporal Hill and I'm not a happy man.'

b4   *'If we have got to have five hundred weighing machines in the house, I'd just as soon they did sing.'*

a5   'He's an oul' butty o'mine–oh, he's a darlin' man, a daarlin' man.'

b5   *'After you, Claude.' 'No, after you, Cecil.'*

a6   'If music be the food of love, play on.'

b6   *'A child of five would understand this. Send somebody to find a child of five.'*

a7   'Describe a circle, stroke its back and it turns vicious.'

b7   *'Come not Lucifer, I'll burn my books.'*

a8   'Midnight, not a sound from the pavement.'

b8   *'Mister Christian!!!!!'*

a9   'Oh, 'tis a glorious thing, I ween
To be a regular Royal Queen.'

b9   *'Here's another fine mess you've gotten me into.'*

a10   'One morning I shot an elephant in my pajamas. How he got into my pajamas I'll never know.'

b10   *'Brazil–where the nuts come from.'*

No. 10 Answers

a1 *Gone With the Wind* (spoken by Clark Gable as Rhett Butler)
b1 The Mikado *by Gilbert and Sullivan*
a2 Mae West in her play *Diamond Lil* and (later) her film *She Done Him Wrong*
b2 *Gwendolen in* The Importance of Being Earnest *by Oscar Wilde*
a3 *Oh What a Lovely War!* by Charles Chilton
b3 *Al Jolson in the film* The Jazz Singer
a4 *Chips with Everything* by Arnold Wesker
b4 One Way Pendulum *by N. F. Simpson*
a5 *Juno and the Paycock* by Sean O'Casey
b5 ITMA *(It's That Man Again) BBC Radio show, by Ted Kavanagh*
a6 Orsino in *Twelfth Night* by William Shakespeare
b6 *Groucho Marx in the film* Duck Soup
a7 *The Bald Prima Donna* by Eugene Ionesco
b7 Doctor Faustus *by Christopher Marlowe*
a8 *Cats* by T. S. Eliot and Andrew Lloyd Webber
b8 *The film* Mutiny on the Bounty
a9 *The Gondoliers* by Gilbert and Sullivan
b9 *Oliver Hardy in several films*
a10 Groucho Marx in the film *Animal Crackers*
b10 *Lord Fancourt in* Charley's Aunt *by Brandon Thomas*

Tie-breaker

Q Which theatrical knight is credited with saying (off-stage), 'The most precious things in speech are pauses'?
A *Sir Ralph Richardson*

No. 11 Double Acts

On the big screen, which acting 'duos' starred in...
a1 *The Graduate?*
b1 Bonnie and Clyde?
a2 *Midnight Cowboy?*
b2 Easy Rider?
a3 *Doctor Zhivago?*
b3 The Sting?
a4 *Love Story?*
b4 The Great Gatsby?
a5 *Grease?*
b5 Last Tango in Paris?

On stage or screen, whose servants are...
a6 Lucky?
b6 *Mary Warren?*
a7 Launcelot Gobbo?
b7 *Dromio of Syracuse?*
a8 Passepartout?
b8 Mrs Bridges?

And in which plays do we meet...
a9 Charles and Elvira?
b9 *George and Martha?*
a10 Grusha and Azdak?
b10 *Pizarro and Atahuallpa?*

No. 11 Answers

a1 Anne Bancroft and Dustin Hoffman
b1 *Warren Beatty and Faye Dunaway*
a2 Jon Voight and Dustin Hoffman
b2 *Dennis Hopper and Peter Fonda*
a3 Omar Sharif and Julie Christie
b3 *Paul Newman and Robert Redford*
a4 Ali MacGraw and Ryan O'Neal
b4 *Mia Farrow and Robert Redford*
a5 John Travolta and Olivia Newton-John
b5 *Marlon Brando and Maria Schneider*
a6 Pozzo's (in *Waiting for Godot* by Samuel Beckett)
b6 *John and Elizabeth Proctor's (in* The Crucible *by Arthur Miller)*
a7 Shylock's and later Bassanio's (in *The Merchant of Venice* by William Shakespeare)
b7 *Antipholus of Syracuse's (in* The Comedy of Errors *by William Shakespeare)*
a8 Phileas Fogg's in *Around the World in Eighty Days*
b8 *The Bellamy family's (in television's* Upstairs, Downstairs*)*
a9 *Blithe Spirit* by Noël Coward
b9 *Who's Afraid of Virginia Woolf? by Edward Albee*
a10 *The Caucasian Chalk Circle* by Bertolt Brecht (Grusha is the faithful servant; Azdak the village judge)
b10 *The Royal Hunt of the Sun by Peter Shaffer (Pizarro is leader of the Spanish; Atahuallpa the sun king of the Incas)*

Tie-breaker

Q Which double act performed this dialogue?
'I'll never forget the first words I spoke in the theatre.'
'What were they?'
' "This way please! Programmes!" '?
A *Morecambe and Wise*

No. 12 Hidden Titles–2

Within each of these dialogues are hidden the titles of eight films. Can you spot the titles and say which star appeared in each group of films?

Team A
(*They are in love and in bed*)
She Darling, darling, it's been seven years since we did this.
He I've been itching to see you again. (*He tries to kiss her*)
She No James, we're not married.
He Let's make it legal. Build our own little love nest.
She (*Giggles*) You don't think we're too old for all that monkey business?
He Nonsense. You're as young as you feel.
She (*Snuggling up to him*) You don't think I'm just after your money?
He I don't care a damn.
She (*Affectionate*) So this how to marry a millionaire.
He Shh–let's make love.
She Under the duvet?
He Some like it hot.

Team B
(*This argumentative couple are American*)
He Your trouble is, you're just a child of these modern times.
She And *you* can't bear to be out of the limelight, not for a single moment.
He You drive off downtown, lured by the city lights.
She While you act like some great dictator or a king–
He In New York? Hah. I don't have the readies.
She So why wait for pay day and miss your chances?
He It's as if you've joined some phoney gold rush.
She Try it. Just try living on easy street, buster.

No. 12 Answers

Team A titles
We're Not Married
Let's Make It Legal
Love Nest
Monkey Business
As Young As You Feel
How to Marry a Millionaire
Let's Make Love
Some Like It Hot
and the star is Marilyn Monroe

Team B titles
Modern Times
Limelight
City Lights
The Great Dictator
A King in New York
Pay Day
The Gold Rush
Easy Street
and the star is Charlie Chaplin

No. 13 Star Billing

On television, who played:
a1 Inspector Morse?
b1 *Mr Bean?*
a2 Beatie?
b2 *Del Boy?*
a3 Victor Meldrew?
b3 *Margaret Meldrew?*
a4 Timothy Lumsden?
b4 *Bergerac?*
a5 Den Watts?
b5 *Lovejoy?*
a6 Mrs Boswell?
b6 *Thomas Sullivan (in* Magnum*)?*
a7 René (in *'Allo 'Allo*)?
b7 *Compo?*
a8 Alf's wife in *Till Death Us Do Part?*
b8 *The scarecrow, Worzel Gummidge?*
a9 The gossip columnist in *Lytton's Diary?*
b9 *The male lead in* The Thorn Birds*?*
a10 Sir Humphrey Appleby in *Yes Minister?*
b10 *Jim Hacker?*
a11 Jeeves (in the 1990–93 series)?
b11 *Bertie Wooster (in the same series)?*
a12 Young Lord Sebastian in *Brideshead Revisited?*
b12 *His father, Lord Marchmain?*

No. 13 Answers

a1	John Thaw
b1	*Rowan Atkinson*
a2	Maureen Lipman (in the BT adverts)
b2	*David Jason*
a3	Richard Wilson
b3	*Annette Crosbie*
a4	Ronnie Corbett
b4	*John Nettles*
a5	Leslie Grantham
b5	*Ian McShane*
a6	Jean Boht
b6	*Tom Selleck*
a7	Gordon Kaye
b7	*Bill Owen*
a8	Dandy Nichols
b8	*Jon Pertwee*
a9	Peter Bowles
b9	*Richard Chamberlain*
a10	Nigel Hawthorne
b10	*Paul Eddington*
a11	Stephen Fry
b11	*Hugh Laurie*
a12	Anthony Andrews
b12	*Laurence Olivier*

Tie-breaker

Q Which husband and wife team starred in *Upstairs, Downstairs; Thomas and Sarah* and *Forever Green*?

A *John Alderton and Pauline Collins*

No. 14 Radio Times

a1 On BBC Radio, who sends a weekly *Letter from America*?

b1 *In which radio serial have we met Mrs Antrobus, Lynda Snell and Sid Perks?*

a2 Which Radio One disc jockey was famous for his daily 'Our Tune' spot?

b2 *The first record played on Radio One in 1967 was by the Move. What was it?*

a3 In which radio comedy show did we meet Eccles, Bluebottle and Moriarty?

b3 *And in which programme did we meet Frisby Dyke, Mrs Mopp and Funf?*

a4 Which radio comedy series featured the HMS Troutbridge?

b4 *And in that show, who played 'Number One'?*

a5 On which radio programme did we meet Rambling Syd Rumpo, Julian and Sandy?

b5 *Who was the only female member of the cast?*

a6 In which radio serial did we meet Dick, Jock and Snowy?

b6 *In which long-running comedy radio programme did Richard Murdoch star with Kenneth Horne?*

a7 During the Second World War, for which musical instrument was Sandy Macpherson famous?

b7 *During the Second World War, why were Alvar Lidell, Frank Phillips and John Snagge household names?*

a8 Which was the first national commercial radio station to broadcast in Britain?

b8 *In which BBC comedy radio show did Bebe Daniels appear with the rest of her family?*

a9 Who was the original presenter of *Desert Island Discs*?

b9 *And, in the Sixties, who presented Sunday's* Pick of the Pops*?*

a10 During the Second World War, which two comediennes played the characters Gert and Daisy?

b10 *Which radio bandleader was famous for his weekly guest night?*

No. 14 Answers

a1 Alistair Cooke
b1 The Archers
a2 Simon Bates
b2 *'Flowers in the Rain'*
a3 *The Goon Show*
b3 ITMA *(It's That Man Again)*
a4 *The Navy Lark*
b4 *Stephen Murray*
a5 *Round the Horne*
b5 *Betty Marsden*
a6 Dick Barton
b6 Much-Binding-in-the-Marsh
a7 Organ; theatre organ
b7 *They were radio newsreaders (accept: announcers)*
a8 Classic FM (Others broadcast *to* Britain)
b8 Life with the Lyons
a9 Roy Plomley
b9 *Alan Freeman*
a10 Elsie and Doris Waters
b10 *Henry Hall*

Tie-breaker

Q What memorable phrase did Commander Tommy Woodrooffe
utter several times on radio in 1937 when describing a Spithead
naval review?
A *'The fleet's lit up' (Many listeners thought he was drunk)*

40

No. 15 Film Scores

In which films do we hear each of the following pieces of music:

a1 'The Yellow Brick Road'?
b1 *'Edelweiss'?*
a2 'Mrs Robinson'?
b2 *'Raindrops Keep Falling on My Head'?*
a3 'Big Spender'?
b3 *'Do Not Forsake Me, O My Darlin"?*
a4 The Harry Lime theme?
b4 *'The Entertainer'?*
a5 'Bright Eyes'?
b5 *'Walking in the Air'?*
a6 'The Trolley Song'?
b6 *'Wanderin' Star'?*
a7 'Some Day My Prince Will Come'?
b7 *'The Roses of Success'?*
a8 '(We're Gonna) Rock Around the Clock' (N.B. its first use in a film)
b8 *'Ride Away'?*
a9 'Dancing on the Ceiling'?
b9 *'I Got Rhythm'?*
a10 'Born to Be Wild'?
b10 *'Stayin' Alive'?*
a11 Adagietto from Mahler's 5th Symphony?
b11 *The Overture to The Thieving Magpie?*
a12 The Warsaw Concerto?
b12 *The Missa Luba?*

No. 15 Answers

a1   *The Wizard of Oz*
b1   The Sound of Music
a2   *The Graduate*
b2   Butch Cassidy and the Sundance Kid
a3   *Sweet Charity*
b3   High Noon
a4   *The Third Man*
b4   The Sting
a5   *Watership Down*
b5   The Snowman
a6   *Meet Me in St Louis*
b6   Paint Your Wagon
a7   *Snow White and the Seven Dwarfs*
b7   Chitty Chitty Bang Bang
a8   *The Blackboard Jungle*
b8   The Searchers
a9   *Evergreen*
b9   An American in Paris
a10 *Easy Rider*
b10 Saturday Night Fever
a11 *Death in Venice*
b11 A Clockwork Orange
a12 *Dangerous Moonlight*
b12 If...

Tie-breaker

Q   The film *Mary Poppins* contains a song with a very long invented word as its title. What is it–and can you spell it?

A   *Supercalifragilisticexpialidocius*

No. 16 Scrambled Shakespeare

This scene is more or less by Shakespeare. Except that he wrote the lines for eight different plays. From which plays do the lines come? (Quiz 17 offers a similar test for an opposing team!)

Lord or Lady
To be or not to be: that is the question–
Whether 'tis nobler in the mind to suffer
The slings and arrows of outrageous fortune
Or close the wall up with our English dead
For now is the Winter of our discontent
Made glorious Summer by this sun of York–
Another Lord or Lady
Yet, my friend, keep up your bright swords,
For the dew will rust them–*et tu*, Brute!
First L.
Yes, if it were done when 'tis done, then 'twere well
It were done quickly–
Second L.
–Alas poor Yorick!
First L.
Indeed, forsooth, Duncan is in his grave!
Second L.
But the quality of mercy is not strained,
Fair is foul and foul is fair.
First L.
Light thickens–
Second L.
In such a night as this
Troilus methinks mounted the Trojan walls
And said, 'Parting is such sweet sorrow.'

No. 16 Answers

[Passages in square brackets are not taken from any particular play.]

To be or not to be: that is the question–
Whether 'tis nobler in the mind to suffer
The slings and arrows of outrageous fortune (*Hamlet*)

Or close the wall up with our English dead (*Henry V*)

For now is the Winter of our discontent
Made glorious Summer by this sun of York (*Richard III*)

[Yet, my friend,] keep up your bright swords,
For the dew will rust them (*Othello*)

–*et tu*, Brute! (*Julius Caesar*)

[Yes,] if it were done when 'tis done, then 'twere well
It were done quickly–(*Macbeth*)

–Alas poor Yorick! (*Hamlet*)

[Indeed, forsooth,] Duncan is in his grave! (*Macbeth*)

[But] the quality of mercy is not strained (*The Merchant of Venice*)

Fair is foul and foul is fair.
Light thickens–(*Macbeth*)

In such a night as this
Troilus methinks mounted the Trojan walls (*The Merchant of Venice*)

[And said,] 'Parting is such sweet sorrow.' (*Romeo and Juliet*)

No. 17 More Scrambled Shakespeare

Like the dialogue in the last round, this scene is by Shakespeare. Except that he wrote the lines for eight different plays. From which plays do these lines come? (See also Quiz No. 16)

Fool
Beware the Ides of March!
For is this a dagger which I see before me,
The handle towards my hand?

Clown
Come, let me clutch thee–

Fool
Ah ha, yes, I have thee.
Now friends, Romans, countrymen, lend me your ears.

Clown
This is the most unkindest cut of all!

Fool
Ah ha–a hit, a very palpable hit!

Clown
Dost thou think because thou are virtuous,
Mewling and puking in thy nurse's arms
And the whining–

Fool
Rumble thy bellyful! Spit, fire! spout, rain!

Clown
The eye of man hath not heard, the ear of man hath not seen, man's hand is not able to taste, his tongue to conceive, nor his heart to report, what thy dream is.

Fool
Prithee, I'll break my staff,
And bury it certain fathoms in the earth–

Clown
Because it hath no bottom?

No. 17 Answers

[Passages in square brackets are not taken from any particular play]

Beware the Ides of March! (*Julius Caesar*)

[For] is this a dagger which I see before me,
The handle towards my hand? Come, let me clutch thee–(*Macbeth*)

[Ah ha, yes, I have thee.]

[Now] friends, Romans, countrymen, lend me your ears.
This is the most unkindest cut of all (*Julius Caesar*)

[Ah ha–] a hit, a very palpable hit! (*Hamlet*)

Dost thou think because thou are virtuous (*Twelfth Night*)

Mewling and puking in thy nurse's arms
And the whining–(*As You Like It*)

Rumble thy bellyful! Spit, fire! spout, rain! (*King Lear*)

The eye of man hath not heard, the ear of man hath not seen, man's
hand is not able to taste, his tongue to conceive, nor his heart to report,
what thy dream is. (*A Midsummer Night's Dream*)

Prithee, I'll break my staff,
And bury it certain fathoms in the earth–(*The Tempest*)

Because it hath no bottom? (*A Midsummer Night's Dream*)

No. 18 Small Screen Stars

a1 In *Dallas*, who played J. R. Ewing?

b1 *Who played Elsie Howard in* Coronation Street*?*

a2 Who played 'the blonde half' of *Starsky and Hutch*?

b2 *Which actor played the manager of the hotel in* Fawlty Towers*?*

a3 Which one-time pop star played a millionaire in *Love Hurts*?

b3 *And of which series were Julie Covington, Charlotte Cornwell and Rula Lenska the stars?*

a4 Who played young Dr Latimer in *Don't Wait Up*?

b4 *Who played Hadleigh in the series of that name?*

a5 Who played the dotty chalet maid in *Hi-de-Hi!*?

b5 *In which comedy series did Judi Dench and Michael Williams star together?*

a6 Which disc jockey created Captain Kremmen?

b6 *With which long-running television series is Jonathan Routh particularly associated?*

a7 Who played the detective Van der Valk?

b7 *Which detective was played by Jack Klugman?*

a8 On which island was *Magnum* set?

b8 *Name the actor who played Kojak on television.*

a9 Which actor played the detective, Cannon?

b9 *And also on television, who played Callan?*

a10 In *Coronation Street*, which character was played by Peter Adamson?

b10 *Which time travellers were played by David McCallum and Joanna Lumley?*

a11 Who played 'The Bounder'?

b11 *Which role did Annette Crosbie play in the series* Edward the Seventh*?*

a12 Who played Francis Urquhart in *House of Cards* and *To Play the King*?

b12 *Who played Eric Sykes' 'sister'?*

No. 18 Answers

a1 Larry Hagman
b1 *Patricia Phoenix*
a2 David Soul ('Hutch')
b2 *John Cleese*
a3 Adam Faith
b3 *Rock Follies*
a4 Nigel Havers
b4 *Gerald Harper*
a5 Su Pollard
b5 *A Fine Romance*
a6 Kenny Everett
b6 *Candid Camera*
a7 Barry Foster
b7 *Quincy*
a8 Hawaii
b8 *Telly Savalas*
a9 William Conrad
b9 *Edward Woodward*
a10 Len Fairclough
b10 *Sapphire and Steel*
a11 Peter Bowles
b11 *Queen Victoria*
a12 Ian Richardson
b12 *Hattie Jacques*

Tie-breaker

Q Who introduced *The Muppet Show*?
A *Kermit (the Frog)*

No. 19 Cinema Classics

a1   Which cartoon cat that never quite manages to catch Tweetie Pie?

b1   *Name the cartoon cat who 'kept on walking'.*

a2   Which child film star sang 'On the good ship lollipop'?

b2   *Buster Keaton played an engine driver in which classic silent film?*

a3   Who came from the planet Krypton?

b3   *In which film studios were the comedies* Passport to Pimlico, Whisky Galore! *and* The Lavender Hill Mob *made?*

a4   About which battle is the film *A Bridge Too Far*?

b4   *The film* Tora! Tora! Tora! *was about an attack on which American base?*

a5   Who played a Mafia leader in *The Godfather* and the hero's father in the 1978 version of *Superman*?

b5   *In which film did Orson Welles play Harry Lime?*

a6   Which couple became famous for their dancing in the films *Top Hat* and *Swing Time*?

b6   *Of which film is 'Somewhere My Love' a theme tune?*

a7   In which film did Robert Shaw play Captain Quint?

b7   *About which year is Stanley Kubrick's film that is sub-titled 'A Space Odyssey'?*

a8   Who was the leading star of the film *Nutcracker*?

b8   *Who starred in the 1976 version of the film* A Star is Born*?*

a9   In which film did John Hurt play the part of the unfortunate real-life character John Merrick?

b9   *His real name was William Pratt but by what name did he became famous for playing Frankenstein's Monster?*

a10   The uncovering of which political scandal is portrayed in the film *All the President's Men*?

b10   *To which century did Buck Rogers travel?*

a11   Who played the title role in the film *Arthur*?

b11   *Neil Diamond made his film début in a re-make of an Al Jolson classic. What is the film called?*

a12   In which film did Ben Kingsley play an advocate of non-violence?

b12   *Which star appeared in drag in* Tootsie*?*

No. 19 Answers

a1 Sylvester
b1 *Felix*
a2 Shirley Temple
b2 The General
a3 Superman
b3 *Ealing*
a4 Arnhem
b4 *Pearl Harbor*
a5 Marlon Brando
b5 The Third Man
a6 Fred Astaire and Ginger Rogers
b6 Dr Zhivago
a7 *Jaws*
b7 2001
a8 Joan Collins
b8 *Kris Kristofferson and Barbra Streisand*
a9 *The Elephant Man*
b9 *Boris Karloff*
a10 Watergate
b10 *25th Century*
a11 Dudley Moore
b11 The Jazz Singer
a12 Gandhi
b12 *Dustin Hoffman*

Tie-breaker

Q Who played the male lead in the film *The Sound of Music?*
A *Christopher Plummer*

No. 20 Where's That From?–2

From which theatrical classics do these quotations come–and who wrote each play?

a1 'Was that the face that launched a thousand ships?'

b1 'A handbag?'

a2 'Walk? Not bloody likely!'

b2 'Where's my serpent of old Nile?'

a3 'She's as headstrong as an allegory on the banks of the Nile.'

b3 'Unsex me here.'

a4 'If only we could get back to Moscow.'

b4 'I'll lug the guts into the neighbour room.'

a5 'Yet we have gone on living, living and partly living.'

b5 'Goats and monkeys!'

a6 'Every time a child says, "I don't believe in fairies", there's a little fairy somewhere that falls down dead.'

b6 'I can resist everything except temptation.'

a7 'I was adored once, too.'

b7 'Stand not upon the order of your going. But go at once.'

a8 'Elle a des idées au-dessus de sa gare.'

b8 'I see you stand like greyhounds in the slips.'

a9 'Very flat, Norfolk.'

b9 'Now I am the ruler of the queen's navy.'

a10 'For this relief much thanks.'

b10 'It was the nightingale and not the lark.'

a11 'Life is rather like a tin of sardines. We're all of us looking for the key.'

b11 'Be not afeard: the isle is full of strange noises.'

a12 'We are all born mad. Some remain so.'

b12 'His name was never in the paper. He's not the finest character that ever lived. But he's a human being, and a terrible thing is happening to him.'

No. 20 Answers

a1 *Doctor Faustus* by Christopher Marlowe
b1 The Importance of Being Earnest *by Oscar Wilde*
a2 *Pygmalion* by George Bernard Shaw
b2 Antony and Cleopatra *by William Shakespeare*
a3 *The Rivals* by R. B. Sheridan
b3 Macbeth *by William Shakespeare*
a4 *Three Sisters* by Anton Chekhov
b4 Hamlet *by William Shakespeare*
a5 *Murder in the Cathedral* by T. S. Eliot
b5 Othello *by William Shakespeare*
a6 *Peter Pan* by J. M. Barrie
b6 Lady Windermere's Fan *by Oscar Wilde*
a7 *Twelfth Night* by William Shakespeare
b7 Macbeth *by William Shakespeare*
a8 *French Without Tears* by Terence Rattigan
b8 Henry V *by William Shakespeare*
a9 *Private Lives* by Noël Coward
b9 HMS Pinafore *by Gilbert and Sullivan*
a10 *Hamlet* by William Shakespeare
b10 Romeo and Juliet *by William Shakespeare*
a11 *Beyond the Fringe* by Alan Bennett
b11 The Tempest *by William Shakespeare*
a12 *Waiting for Godot* by Samuel Beckett
b12 Death of a Salesman *by Arthur Miller*

Tie-breaker

Q Who gave this advice to a young actor: 'My dear boy, forget about the motivation: just say your lines and don't trip over the furniture'?

A *Noël Coward*

No. 21 The West End–and Beyond

What are the surnames of these theatrical knights and ladies...
a1 ...Sir John?
b1 ...*Sir Ralph?*
a2 ...Dame Flora?
b2 ...*Dame Judi?*
a3 ...Sir Michael?
b3 ...*Dame Edith?*
a4 ...Dame Peggy?
b4 ...*Sir Ian?*

Which show...
a5 ...is a Lloyd Webber musical based on a Billy Wilder musical?
b5 ...*involves a group of English holiday-makers ski-ing (on stage)?*
a6 ...is about a group of people watching televised soccer?
b6 ...*starred Jason Donovan and then Phillip Schofield when it was revived in the West End?*
a7 ...is a David Mamet play about 'politically correct' language and behaviour?
b7 ...*is a Willy Russell play about a bored housewife?*

In London, who originally played the role of...
a8 ...Denis Thatcher in *Anyone for Denis?*
b8 ...*George III in* The Madness of George III?
a9 ...The witch in *Into the Woods?*
b9 ...*Jeffrey Barnard in* Jeffrey Barnard is Unwell?

Who wrote...
a10 ...*Bouncers, Shakers* and *Teechers?*
b10 ...*Educating Rita?*
a11 ...*Saved?*
b11 ...*Dancing at Lughnasa?*
a12 ...*Torch Song Trilogy?*
b12 ...*Lettuce and Lovage?*

No. 21 Answers

a1   Gielgud or Mills
b1   *Richardson*
a2   Robson
b2   *Dench*
a3   Redgrave
b3   *Evans*
a4   Ashcroft
b4   *McKellen*
a5   *Sunset Boulevard*
b5   On the Piste
a6   *An Evening With Gary Lineker*
b6   Joseph and the Amazing Technicolor Dreamcoat
a7   *Oleanna*
b7   Shirley Valentine
a8   John Wells
b8   *Nigel Hawthorne*
a9   Julia McKenzie
b9   *Peter O'Toole*
a10   John Godber
b10   *Willy Russell*
a11   Edward Bond
b11   *Brian Friel*
a12   Harvey Fierstein
b12   *Peter Shaffer*

Tie-breaker

Q   Which mime artist and actor presented and starred in the controversial shows *Flowers* and *Salomé?*
A   *Lindsey Kemp*

No. 22 Hidden Titles–3

In this round, the 'hidden titles' are all of films that were world box office hits in the Eighties. Can you spot the nine film titles concealed in each dialogue?

Team A

(He is plaintive, pleading; she has heard it all before)

He Listen honey, I'd really like to help in the kitchen but I've–

She You've no idea what parenthood involves. You'll get out of anything any which way you can.

He But you know that when I use a machine, the gremlins seem to take over.

She Don't play your war games with me.

He But remember last time I did the washing honey? I shrunk the kids' shirts and the colours ran–

She This is your lethal weapon, isn't it? Incompetence!

He Those trousers are now pink. They're meant to be the color purple.

She God's my witness, I'll make you do something–

He Let me off. Just this once. I'll never say never again.

Team B

(An old-fashioned hero and his wide-eyed girlfriend have been ship wrecked)

Girlfriend This sand! This heat! We're stranded like aliens on a desert island!

Hero But we got out of Africa, my tootsie-wootsie.

Girlfriend I feel we're trapped in some sort of time warp–

Hero We'll get back. To the future, if that's how you think of it. Anyway, I've something to show you.

Girlfriend With your fatal attractions, staying alive is easy.

Hero Now look who's talking! That's better!

Girlfriend What is it?

Hero It's private. For your eyes only. Here.

Girlfriend It's a photograph. Of my pet rabbit.

Hero I thought you'd like it.

Girlfriend But darling, on a desert island, who framed Roger Rabbit?

No. 22 Answers

Team A titles
Parenthood
Any Which Way You Can
Gremlins
War Games
Honey I Shrunk the Kids
Lethal Weapon
The Color Purple
Witness
Never Say Never Again

Team B titles
Aliens (the sequel to the 1979 film *Alien*)
Out of Africa
Tootsie
Back to the Future (a trilogy)
Fatal Attraction
Staying Alive
Look Who's Talking
For Your Eyes Only
Who Framed Roger Rabbit?

No. 23 Funny Business

A round of questions about television 'sitcoms' (or 'situation comedies')

a1 Which family featured in *Bread*?
b1 *Who wrote the series?*
a2 Which son was a poet?
b2 *What was the daughter's first name?*
a3 What was the mother's first name?
b3 *Who had a sandwich business?*
a4 In *Last of the Summer Wine*, who was played by Brian Wilde?
b4 *Who was played by Peter Sallis?*
a5 Which character was the object of Compo's affections?
b5 *Which former* Coronation Street *actress played Auntie Wainwright?*
a6 In *Open All Hours*, who played Arkwright?
b6 *What was the name of his assistant?*
a7 Who played him?
b7 *What was the name of the nurse to whom Arkwright was attracted?*
a8 Who has played (in different series) Rodney and Ashley?
b8 *In which series was he called Ashley and living with a girlfriend?*
a9 What was Rodney's (and Del Boy's) surname?
b9 *And also in that series, who played Grandad?*
a10 In *Fawlty Towers*, who played Sybil?
b10 *And who played Manuel?*
a11 Who played Jacko in *Brush Strokes* and an odd-job man in *Mulberry*?
b11 *Who starred with Geoffrey Palmer in* As Time Goes By?
a12 In which series did Maureen Lipman play a problem page writer?
b12 *And which American sitcom featured the Tates and the Campbells?*

No. 23 Answers

a1 The Boswells
b1 *Carla Lane*
a2 Adrian
b2 *Aveline*
a3 Nellie
b3 *Billy*
a4 Foggy
b4 *(Norman) Clegg*
a5 Nora Batty
b5 *Jean Alexander ('Hilda Ogden')*
a6 Ronnie Barker
b6 *Granville*
a7 David Jason
b7 *Nurse Gladys Emmanuel*
a8 Nicholas Lyndhurst
b8 The Two of Us
a9 Trotter (in *Only Fools and Horses*)
b9 *Leonard Pearce*
a10 Prunella Scales
b10 *Andrew Sachs*
a11 Karl Howman
b11 *(Dame) Judi Dench*
a12 Agony
b12 Soap

Tie-breaker

Q Which television serial featured a wedding reception, a dentists' dance, an angling club's Christmas party and the Miss Cock-a-Doodle Chicken competition?

A A Bit of a Do

No. 24 Your Own, Your Very Own...

The following are all catch phrases of popular stand-up comedians or other entertainers. Who used (or still uses) each phrase?

a1 'Rock on, Tommy'?

b1 *'Just like that'?*

a2 'Not a lot'?

b2 *'Stop messing about'?*

a3 'Bye Jove, I needed that'?

b3 *'A good idea, son!'?*

a4 'Possums'?

b4 *'I'm free'?*

a5 'Give order, thank you please'?

b5 *'Shut that door'?*

a6 'You can't see the join'?

b6 *'The day war broke out...'?*

a7 'Hello playmates'?

b7 *'Can you hear me mother?'?*

a8 'Pin back your lugholes'?

b8 *'Aye, aye, that's yer lot'?*

a9 'I won't take me coat off, I'm not stopping'?

b9 *'Right monkey!'?*

a10 'Hello, my darlings'?

b10 *'Wake up at the back there'?*

a11 'Now there's a funny thing'?

b11 *'It's the way I tell them'?*

a12 'Play the game, cads'?

b12 *'She knows, you know'?*

No. 24 Answers

a1 Bobby Ball (to Tommy Cannon)
b1 *Tommy Cooper*
a2 Paul Daniels
b2 *Kenneth Williams*
a3 Ken Dodd (after a burst on the banjo)
b3 *Max Bygraves*
a4 Barry Humphries (as Dame Edna Everage)
b4 *John Inman*
a5 Colin Crompton
b5 *Larry Grayson*
a6 Eric Morecambe
b6 *Robb Wilton*
a7 Arthur Askey
b7 *Sandy Powell*
a8 Cyril Fletcher
b8 *Jimmy Wheeler*
a9 Ken Platt
b9 *Al Read*
a10 Charlie Drake
b10 *Jimmy Edwards*
a11 Max Miller
b11 *Frank Carson*
a12 The Western Brothers
b12 *Hylda Baker (about 'Cynthia')*

Tie-breaker

Q Which entertainer regularly got laughs with such phrases as 'Ladies and Gentlemen' 'Ere, mush' and 'I was amazed'?

A *Frankie Howerd*

No. 25 Get the Guest–2

How many clues do you need before you can identify each of the following stars of the screen? (See page 9)

Guest A
1 I am the daughter of an American diplomat but studied acting in London.
2 One of my first screen roles was as a villainess in the soap opera *The Doctors*.
3 I have been the husky voice of a very sexy rabbit.
4 I have played the private eye V.I. Warshawski.

Guest B
1 At the age of three, I played a bare-bottomed child in a sun-tan lotion commercial.
2 Always precocious, before the age of 15 played a speak-easy vamp.
3 I have earned a BA in Literature from Yale and an Oscar for playing a rape victim.
4 In 1991, I was involved with Hannibal Lecter.

Guest C
1 After serving in the US Navy, I worked as a nightclub comic.
2 I have been much involved with children's education television and have written manuals on being a parent.
3 My first television role (as a secret agent in the series *I Spy*) made me a household name.
4 I have recorded more than 20 albums and now star in a comedy show named after me.

Guest D
1 I hosted a youth talent show and then became a stand-up comic.
2 My comedy act is not the cleanest; nor is my language–but I've a name for fast-talking satire.
3 My film début lasted 48 hours and I've traded places as a hustler.
4 My best-known screen role is as a Detroit cop working in Beverly Hills.

No. 25 Answers

Guest A Kathleen Turner (1954–)
After appearing in commercials, she was hired as villainess Nola Dancy Aldrich for the television soap-opera The Doctors (1978–80). Her stardom became assured with the popular adventure Romancing the Stone (1984) in which she gave a gutsy performance as a romantic novelist. More recently, she provided the vocal accompaniment to animated bombshell Jessica Rabbit in Who Framed Roger Rabbit? (1988) and starred in V.I. Warshawski (1991) in which she plays a private eye.

Guest B Jodie Foster (1962–)
Her career began at the age of three when she was chosen as the barebottom child in the Coppertone sun tan lotion commercials. She had starring roles in Bugsy Malone and Taxi Driver (both 1976). She gave a harrowing performance as a rape victim in search of justice in The Accused (1988), which won her a Best Actress Oscar. She has since starred in Silence of the Lambs (1991).

Guest C Bill Cosby (1937–)
After serving in the US Navy (1956–60), Cosby enrolled at Temple University, Philadelphia. An appearance on The Tonight Show in 1965 led to his being cast as secret agent Alexander Scott in the television series I Spy (1965–68). He has been involved with children's educational television for many years and his series The Cosby Show (1984–) has consistently topped the ratings.

Guest D
Eddie Murphy (1961–)
His film début was as a fast-talking con in the comedy thriller 48 HRS (1982) and later he played a street-smart hustler in Trading Places (1983). He had the title role of a Detroit cop in Beverly Hills Cop (1984).

No. 26 Nights at the Ballet

Which ballet is being described in each of these questions–and to whose music is it danced?

a1 In Act Two, Prince Florimund is out hunting with his courtiers in the forest. His companions leave to hunt a wild boar and, while he is alone, a fairy tells him of an enchanted castle...?

b1 *She changes into a beautiful girl, wearing a crown. Siegfried goes to her but she tries to flee. He means no harm, he says. She says she is an enchanted princess...?*

a2 The story of two feuding families, the Montagues and the Capulets...?

b2 *Two ugly stepsisters expect her to stay at home while they go to the ball...?*

a3 During the Butterweek Fair in St Petersburg, the owner of a puppet theatre brings two of his puppets to life...?

b3 *As the curtain rises, he pushes into the window his newest creation–a mechanical doll which is so lifelike he believes people will think she is a real person...?*

a4 The President is giving a Christmas party for his small son and daughter, Fritz and Clara. The children are given presents from the Christmas tree and then another guest arrives. He is Herr Drosselmeyer who has bought four clockwork toys...?

b4 *A one-act ballet with no narrative but it is often performed in the setting of a ruined monastery over which the moon throws a silvery light. It was originally danced to five piano pieces...?*

a5 From a hillside, one sunny afternoon, a creature sees seven nymphs in the valley below. When he goes towards them, they run away, but soon return...?

b5 *Prince Ivan captures a bird. In order to gain her release, the bird gives Ivan a feather with which he can call her in moments of danger...?*

a6 A game of love and death, acted out according to the rules of chess...?

b6 *Danced to music originally composed as a setting for a group of poems by Edith Sitwell, this ballet includes a 'Yodelling Song', a 'Scotch Rhapsody' and a 'Popular Song'...?*

No. 26 Answers

a1 *The Sleeping Beauty*; music by Tchaikovsky
b1 Swan Lake*; music by Tchaikovsky*
a2 *Romeo and Juliet*; music by Prokofiev
b2 Cinderella*; music by Prokofiev*
a3 *Petrushka*; music by Stravinsky
b3 Coppélia*; music by Delibes*
a4 *The Nutcracker*; music by Tchaikovsky
b4 Les Sylphides*; music by Chopin*
a5 L'Après-midi d'un Faune (The Afternoon of a Faun); music by Debussy
b5 The Firebird*; music by Stravinsky*
a6 *Checkmate*; music by Arthur Bliss
b6 Façade*; music by William Walton*

Tie-breaker

Q To whose music are these ballets danced:	A
A Midsummer Night's Dream?	*Mendelssohn*
Carmen?	*Bizet*
Spartacus?	*Khachaturian*
Onegin?	*Tchaikovsky*
The Prodigal Son?	*Prokofiev*
The Three Cornered Hat?	*de Falla*

No. 27 Stage Door Chat

a1   What is the name of the theatrical profession's weekly newspaper?

b1   *What is the name of the actors' directory (which they hope will lead to their being cast in new productions)?*

a2   Which Sheffield theatre has become famous as a venue for snooker tournaments?

b2   *Which theatre opened in 1932 with performances of Shakespeare's* Henry IV*?*

a3   Which comedian used his own song 'Confidentially' as his signature tune?

b3   *What was* Oh! Calcutta!*?*

a4   What is 'drying'?

b4   *What is 'corpsing'?*

a5   Which long-running Shavian musical closed in 1963?

b5   *In which London theatre did it play?*

a6   Which actress (who starred in the film *A Passage to India*) has a theatre named after her in Croydon?

b6   *Who was the first director of Britain's National Theatre (and has a theatre named after him)?*

a7   Which was the longest-running musical on the London stage in the Sixties?

b7   *In 1971, Anthony Marriott and Alistair Foot wrote a long-running sex farce–called...what?*

a8   Lord Rix (formerly Brian Rix) was leading man at which London theatre?

b8   *Which actor played Henry VII, Captain Bligh and the Hunchback of Notre Dame?*

a9   Which Terence Rattigan play features a translation by the poet Robert Browning of a Greek text?

b9   *As which Shakespearian tragic hero did Paul Scofield triumph in 1962?*

a10   By what name was the stage revue *The Follies of 1907* popularly known?

b10   *As what did Harry Tate and 'Little Tich' become famous?*

No. 27 Answers

a1   *The Stage (and Television Today)*
b1   Spotlight
a2   The Crucible
b2   *Shakespeare Memorial Theatre, Stratford upon Avon*
a3   Reg Dixon
b3   *Nude revue (1970)*
a4   Forgetting your lines on stage
b4   *Getting the giggles on stage; breaking into laughter at the wrong moment*
a5   *My Fair Lady*
b5   *Theatre Royal, Drury Lane*
a6   Dame Peggy Ashcroft
b6   *Sir Laurence Olivier (later, Lord Olivier)*
a7   *Oliver!*
b7   No Sex Please–We're British
a8   Whitehall Theatre
b8   *Charles Laughton*
a9   *The Browning Version*
b9   King Lear
a10 *The Ziegfeld Follies* (named after Florenz Ziegfeld, the producer)
b10 *Music hall artists*

Tie-breaker

Q By what name were Nervo and Knox, Naughton and Gold, and Flanagan and Allen known when they appeared together on stage?

A *The Crazy Gang*

No. 28 Series and Serials

In which long-running television series and serials have we regularly seen the following characters:

a1 Mike Baldwin?

b1 *Dolly Skilbeck?*

a2 Mrs Bucket (pronounced 'Bouquet')?

b2 *Sharon and Tracey?*

a3 Edina and Patsy?

b3 *Mrs Kiki Frog?*

a4 Doyle and Bodie?

b4 *Detective Chief Inspector Barlow?*

a5 Gladys, Spike and Ted?

b5 *Sam Malone, Norm, Cliffy and Carla?*

a6 Mrs Fforbes-Hamilton?

b6 *Joey, Adrian and our Aveline?*

a7 A solicitor from Pinner called Alec?

b7 *Sandra and Carol?*

a8 Doris, Bruno and Miss Sherwood?

b8 *Roy, Cliff and Donna?*

a9 Nellie Mangel?

b9 *Adam Chance?*

a10 James, Siegfried and Helen?

b10 *Detective Chief Supt Lockhart?*

a11 Jamie McCrimmon, Davros and K9?

b11 *Bingo, Snorky and Drooper?*

a12 Sister Carole Young and Dr Chris Anderson?

b12 *Napoleon Solo?*

No. 28 Answers

a1 *Coronation Street*
b1 Emmerdale Farm
a2 *Keeping Up Appearances*
b2 Birds of a Feather
a3 *Absolutely Fabulous*
b3 Hector's House
a4 *The Professionals*
b4 Z-Cars
a5 *Hi-de-Hi!*
b5 Cheers
a6 *To the Manor Born*
b6 Bread
a7 *May to December*
b7 The Liver Birds
a8 *Fame*
b8 Dallas
a9 *Neighbours*
b9 Crossroads
a10 *All Creatures Great and Small*
b10 No Hiding Place
a11 *Dr Who*
b11 Banana Splits
a12 *Emergency–Ward 10*
b12 The Man From U.N.C.L.E.

Tie-breaker

Q In which television serial did we meet the characters Sarah Layton and Guy Perron?
A Jewel in the Crown

No. 29 Cartoon Time

a1 In cartoon films, who regularly says, 'What's up, Doc?'?

b1 And who says 'I taut I taw a puddy tat'?

a2 What kind of animal is Babar?

b2 Which pirate captain was always under attack from Cut Throat Jake?

a3 What was the name of the 'man-cub' in *The Jungle Book*?

b3 What was Popeye's girlfriend called?

a4 Which vegetable did he eat for strength?

b4 Of whose gang was Choo-Choo a member?

a5 What was the Flintstones' home town?

b5 What was the name of their family pet?

a6 What kind of dog is Scooby Doo?

b6 Which scientist found a way of going backwards in time? (A cartoon one, remember)

a7 Which character played the Sorcerer's Apprentice in the film *Fantasia*?

b7 In which Disney film do two dogs dine out at an Italian restaurant?

a8 Which cartoon character appeared in a number of films involving Inspector Clouseau (played by Peter Sellers)?

b8 Which short-sighted old gentleman had a nephew called Waldo?

a9 With which real-life actor did Jerry (of Tom and Jerry) dance in *Anchors Away*?

b9 Which partnership (later a company) created Tom and Jerry, Yogi Bear and the Flintstones?

a10 With which cartoon characters did 'Father Abraham' hit the pop charts?

b10 Who narrated Roobarb and Custard?

a11 Which 1993 cartoon environmental saga was a European Broadcasting Union co-production?

b11 And which cartoon project (also of the early Nineties) was a joint Welsh and Russian project?

a12 Who were Huey, Dewey and Louie?

b12 In which feature-length cartoon was the song 'Little April Shower'?

No. 29 Answers

a1	Bugs Bunny
b1	*Tweetie Pie*
a2	An elephant
b2	*Pugwash*
a3	Mowgli
b3	*Olive Oyl*
a4	Spinach
b4	*Top Cat's (TC) (He has also been known as Boss Cat)*
a5	Bedrock
b5	*Dino*
a6	A Great Dane
b6	*Hector Heathcote*
a7	Mickey Mouse
b7	The Lady and the Tramp
a8	The Pink Panther
b8	*Mr Magoo*
a9	Gene Kelly
b9	*Hanna Barbera (William Hanna and Joe Barbera)*
a10	The Smurfs
b10	*Richard Briers*
a11	*The Animals of Farthing Wood*
b11	Tales from Shakespeare
a12	Donald Duck's nephews
b12	Bambi

Tie-breaker

Q Of whom did Alfred Hitchcock say, 'He has the best casting. If he doesn't like an actor, he just tears him up'?

A *Walt Disney*

No. 30 Dramatis Personae–1

In which play would you encounter the following characters–and who wrote each play?

a1   Stephano and Trinculo?

b1   *Big Daddy?*

a2   Stanhope, Osborne and Raleigh (in the trenches of the First World War)?

b2   *The two 'harmless' old dears, Abby and Martha Brewster?*

a3   Pierce (or Piers) de Gaveston?

b3   *The Austrian composer Salieri?*

a4   Tituba and Deputy Governor Danforth?

b4   *Calpurnia?*

a5   Hester Collyer and ex-RAF pilot Freddie Page?

b5   *Norman and 'Sir'?*

a6   Frank and Rita?

b6   *Florizel?*

a7   A six-foot tall white rabbit?

b7   *Sergeant Mitcham, Private Bamforth and a Japanese soldier?*

a8   Célimène and the rather grumpy Alceste?

b8   *Costard?*

a9   Helen, her daughter Jo, and Geoffrey?

b9   *Julius Winterhalter and the Lancaster family?*

a10   Dromio of Ephesus?

b10   *Young Siward?*

a11   Thomas More and Richard Rich?

b11   *Sir Peter and Lady Teazle?*

a12   Bluntschli, the 'chocolate soldier'?

b12   *The Dauphin, Chaplain de Stogumber and Dunois, Bastard of Orleans?*

No. 30 Answers

a1 *The Tempest* by William Shakespeare
b1 Cat on a Hot Tin Roof *by Tennessee Williams*
a2 *Journey's End* by R. C. Sherriff
b2 Arsenic and Old Lace *by Joseph Kesselring*
a3 *Edward II* by Marlowe
b3 Amadeus *by Peter Shaffer*
a4 *The Crucible* by Arthur Miller
b4 Julius Caesar *by William Shakespeare*
a5 *The Deep Blue Sea* by Terence Rattigan
b5 The Dresser *by Ronald Harwood*
a6 *Educating Rita* by Willy Russell
b6 The Winter's Tale *by William Shakespeare*
a7 *Harvey* by Mary Chase
b7 The Long and the Short and the Tall *by Willis Hall*
a8 *The Misanthrope* by Molière
b8 Love's Labour's Lost *by William Shakespeare*
a9 *A Taste of Honey* by Shelagh Delaney
b9 Waters of the Moon *by N. C. Hunter*
a10 *The Comedy of Errors* by William Shakespeare
b10 Macbeth *by William Shakespeare*
a11 *A Man for All Seasons* by Robert Bolt
b11 The School for Scandal *by R. B. Sheridan*
a12 *Arms and the Man* by George Bernard Shaw
b12 Saint Joan *by George Bernard Shaw*

Tie-breaker

Q In which of Tom Stoppard's plays are there characters called Thomasina Coverly, Septimus Hodge and Bernard Nightingale?

A Arcadia

No. 31 Best Actors

Who won an Oscar for Best Actor with the following films:

a1   *The Godfather* (1972)?
b1   My Fair Lady *(1964)?*
a2   *One Flew Over the Cuckoo's Nest* (1975)?
b2   True Grit *(1969)?*
a3   *Ben-Hur* (1959)?
b3   Bridge on the River Kwai *(1957)?*
a4   *On Golden Pond* (1981)?
b4   The King and I *(1956)?*
a5   *Network* (1976)?
b5   Patton *(1970)?*
a6   *The Kiss of the Spiderwoman* (1985)?
b6   In the Heat of the Night *(1967)?*
a7   *My Left Foot* (1989)?
b7   To Kill a Mockingbird *(1962)?*
a8   *Wall Street* (1987)?
b8   Elmer Gantry *(1960)?*
a9   *High Noon* (1952)?
b9   Reversal of Fortune *(1990)?*
a10   *Separate Tables* (1958)?
b10   Hamlet *(1948)?*
a11   *The Private Life of Henry VIII* (1932–33)?
b11   Yankee Doodle Dandy *(1942)?*
a12   *Goodbye Mr Chips* (1939)?
b12   The Best Years of Our Lives *(1946)?*

No. 31 Answers

a1 Marlon Brando (although awarded the Oscar, he refused to accept it)

b1 *Rex Harrison*

a2 Jack Nicholson

b2 *John Wayne*

a3 Charlton Heston

b3 *Alec Guinness*

a4 Henry Fonda

b4 *Yul Brynner*

a5 Peter Finch

b5 *George C. Scott (although awarded the Oscar, he refused to accept it)*

a6 William Hurt

b6 *Rod Steiger*

a7 Daniel Day-Lewis

b7 *Gregory Peck*

a8 Michael Douglas

b8 *Burt Lancaster*

a9 Gary Cooper

b9 *Jeremy Irons*

a10 David Niven

b10 *Laurence Olivier*

a11 Charles Laughton

b11 *James Cagney*

a12 Robert Donat

b12 *Frederic March*

Tie-breaker

Q Which Academy awards the Oscars?

A *The American Academy of Motion Picture Arts and Sciences*

No. 32 Hidden Titles–4

Within each of these dialogues are hidden the titles of nine songs from stage or screen musicals. Can you spot the song titles, say which show they each come from *and* who wrote each group of shows?

Team A

Frightened man I'm frightened. Tonight, I'm really frightened.

Powerful Lady There's nothing to be afraid of. Not while I'm around.

Man Listen! I feel pretty sure something's coming.

Lady You're safe. No one is alone you know. We're sitting side by side. (*Pause*) By side.

Man Johanna, I'm still afraid.

Lady Later you can watch the television. I think there's a comedy tonight.

Man I'll need more than that.

Lady In that case, when I go, I can easily send in the clowns.

Team B

(*Two fitness freaks wake up one morning...*)

1 Hey, are you awake, Superstar?

2 (*Waking*) What's up?

1 Everything's all right.

2 I was right out.

1 You were tired, man. After an evening pumping iron.

2 Well, I closed my eyes, drew back the curtain and I was away.

1 Well, all I ask of you now is you get up.

2 OK

1 Any memory of your dreams?

2 Gone. All gone. Just like the music of the night.

1 That's real poetic.

2 No, wait. There was a light.

1 A light?

2 A light at the end of the tunnel, my love.

1 'Love'? Well, love changes everything.

No. 32 Answers

Team A titles
'Tonight' from *West Side Story*
'Not While I'm Around' from *Sweeney Todd–The Demon Barber of Fleet Street*
'I Feel Pretty' from *West Side Story*
'Something's Coming' from *West Side Story*
'No one is Alone' from *Into the Woods*
'Side by Side by Side' from *Company*
'Johanna' from *Sweeney Todd–The Demon Barber of Fleet Street*
'Comedy Tonight' from *A Funny Thing Happened on the Way to the Forum*
'Send in the Clowns' from *A Little Night Music*
and they were all written by Stephen Sondheim

Team B titles
'Superstar' from *Jesus Christ Superstar*
'Everything's All Right' from *Jesus Christ Superstar*
'Pumping Iron' from *Starlight Express*
'I Closed My Eyes, Drew Back the Curtain' from *Joseph and the Amazing Technicolor Dreamcoat*
'All I Ask of You' from *The Phantom of the Opera*
'Memory' from *Cats*
'The Music of the Night' from *The Phantom of the Opera*
'Light at the End of the Tunnel' from *Starlight Express*
'Love Changes Everything' from *Aspects of Love*
and they were all composed by Andrew Lloyd Webber

No. 33 Odd One Out–1

Team A
Here are three speeches which sound as if they might have been written by Shakespeare–but only two are genuine. Which is the impostor–and do you know where the true ones come from?

Shakespearian Speech 1
Titus   The hunt is up, the moon is bright and grey,
The fields are fragrant, and the woods are green,
Uncouple here, and let us make a bay,
And wake the Emperor, and his lovely bride,
And rouse the prince, and ring a hunter's peal,
That all the court may echo with the noise.
Sons, let it be your charge, as it is ours,
To attend the emperor's person carefully.

Shakespearian Speech 2
Constance O, if thou teach me to believe this sorrow,
Teach thou this sorrow how to make me die!
And let belief and life encounter so
As doth the fury of two desperate men
Which in the very meeting fall and die.
Lewis marry Blanche! O boy, then where art thou?
France friend with England, what becomes of me?

Shakespearian Speech 3
King   Not so, good Westmoreland, so wan with care;
We know thou lov'st our royal person true,
With greater grace than office doth demand,
And we shall be thy friend again and thou be ours!
Raise up thy head, thou very straightest plant
In this sad forest of intrigue and sin
Where Northumberland and saucy Worcester,
Malevolent to us in all aspects,
Contrive against our throne.

Team B

Here are three speeches which might or might not have been written by the Russian dramatist, Anton Chekhov. Which is the impostor–and from which plays or playlets do the other two come?

Chekhov Speech 1

My wife runs a school of music, I might add, and a private boarding school–well, not a boarding school exactly but something in that line. Between you and me, my wife likes to complain of being hard up, but she's got a tidy bit salted away–while I haven't a penny to my name, not a bean. I'm the school matron. I buy food, keep an eye on the servants, do the accounts, make up exercise books, exterminate bed-bugs, take the wife's dog for walks and catch mice.

Chekhov Speech 2

It's warm today and we can have the windows wide open, but the birch trees aren't in leaf yet. It's 11 years now since father got his brigade and we all left Moscow. I remember it so well. It was early May, as it is now, and in Moscow everything was in blossom, it was warm and there was sunshine everywhere. Eleven years ago, but I remember it all as though we'd only left yesterday.

Chekhov Speech 3

It was in this nursery that I slept and woke each morning to a day of happiness, playing with old Sasha. And at night there were parties with music and singing by the lake. The estate was well kept up then of course. Now we haven't the roubles to pay Ilya Ilyich and the estate must be auctioned. I'm nearly 43 and I must leave–but I shall leave like an officer. There may be a weight upon my heart but country life, I shall say, doesn't really suit me. A bird is judged by its flight.

(Answers on page 253)

No. 34 I Wish I'd Said That!

With which television shows are these sayings or catch phrases associated?

a1 'To boldly go...'?
b1 *'Exterminate, exterminate!'?*
a2 'Ooh, Betty!'?
b2 *'Silly old moo!'?*
a3 'Wink, wink, nudge, nudge, say no more'?
b3 *'Permission to speak, sir!'?*
a4 'Anthea, give us a twirl'?
b4 *'I mean that most sincerely, friends'?*
a5 'Open the box!'?
b5 *'Your starter for ten'?*
a6 'I only arsked'?
b6 *'You dirty old man'?*
a7 'I'm free!'?
b7 *'Bernie, the bolt'?*
a8 'Very interesting...but stupid'?
b8 *'Kissy, kissy'?*
a9 'Evening all!'?
b9 *'And the same question to Number 2'?*
a10 'Sticky-backed plastic'?
b10 *'Everybody out'?*
a11 'Magic!'?
b11 *'Qué?'?*
a12 'I didn't get where I am today...'?
b12 *'Just the facts, ma'am'?*

No. 34 Answers

a1 *Star Trek*
b1 Dr Who *(the Daleks)*
a2 *Some Mothers Do Have 'Em* (Michael Crawford)
b2 Till Death Us Do Part *(Warren Mitchell as Alf Garnett)*
a3 *Monty Python's Flying Circus* (Eric Idle)
b3 Dad's Army *(Clive Dunn as Lance-Corporal Jones)*
a4 *The Generation Game* (Bruce Forsyth)
b4 Opportunity Knocks *(Hughie Greene)*
a5 *Take Your Pick* (introduced by Michael Miles; it was the audience who shouted the advice)
b5 University Challenge *(Bamber Gascoigne)*
a6 *The Army Game* (Bernard Bresslaw)
b6 Steptoe and Son *(Harry H. Corbett)*
a7 *Are You Being Served?* (John Inman)
b7 The Golden Shot *(Bob Monkhouse)*
a8 *Rowan and Martin's Laugh-In*
b8 The Muppet Show *(Miss Piggy)*
a9 *Dixon of Dock Green* (Jack Warner, playing PC George Dixon)
b9 Blind Date
a10 *Blue Peter*
b10 The Rag Trade *(Miriam Karlin)*
a11 *Oh No, It's Selwyn Froggit* (Bill Maynard)
b11 Fawlty Towers *(Andrew Sachs as Manuel)*
a12 *The Fall and Rise of Reginald Perrin* (said by 'C. J.')
b12 Dragnet

Tie-breaker

Q On which show did Janice Nicholls often say, 'I'll give it foive'?
A Thank Your Lucky Stars

No. 35 Your Tiny Hand Is Frozen

From which opera do these come (and who wrote each opera)?

a1   'Your Tiny Hand Is Frozen'?
b1   *'Nessun Dorma'?*
a2   The Chorus of the Hebrew Slaves?
b2   *The Anvil Chorus?*
a3   'Figaro here, Figaro there'?
b3   *The Toreador's Song?*
a4   'Love and music, these I have lived for' or 'Vissi d'arte'?
b4   *'One fine day'?*
a5   The Magic Fire music?
b5   *The Grand March?*
a6   The Willow Song?
b6   *'La donna è mobile'?*
a7   'Pa-pa-pa-pa-pa-pa-pa...'?
b7   *The Bridal Chorus?*
a8   The Trojan March?
b8   *The Jewel Song?*
a9   The Catalogue Song and the Champagne Aria?
b9   *The Letter Duet?*
a10   'The Flight of the Bumble Bee'?
b10   *The drinking song 'Libiamo, libiamo ne' lieti calici' ('Let's drink from the wine-cup o'erflowing')?*
a11   'Recondita armonia' ('Strange harmony of contrasts')?
b11   *'The Hindu Song' (otherwise 'The Song of the Indian Merchant')?*
a12   'Oh star of eve' ('O du mein holder Abendstern')?
b12   *'Did Not a Tear Unwillingly...'('Una furtiva lagrima')?*

No. 35 Answers

a1   *La Bohème* (*Bohemian Life*) by Puccini
b1   Turandot *by Puccini*
a2   *Nabucco* by Verdi
b2   Il Trovatore *(The Troubadour) by Verdi*
a3   *Il Barbiere di Siviglia* (*The Barber of Seville*) by Rossini
b3   Carmen *by Bizet*
a4   *Tosca* by Puccini
b4   Madame Butterfly *by Puccini*
a5   *Die Walküre* (*The Valkyrie*; accept: *The Ring*) by Wagner
b5   Aida *by Verdi*
a6   *Otello* by Verdi
b6   Rigoletto *by Verdi*
a7   *Die Zauberflöte* (*The Magic Flute*) by Mozart (The duet 'Papageno')
b7   Lohengrin *by Wagner*
a8   *Les Trogens* (*The Trojans*) by Berlioz
b8   Faust *by Gounod*
a9   Both from *Don Giovanni* by Mozart (The Catalogue Song–'Madamina, il catalogo'–is a list of Don Giovanni's 'conquests'; the Champagne Aria is Don Giovanni's solo aria, in which he plans a party)
b9   Le Nozze di Figaro *(The Marriage of Figaro) by Mozart*
a10   *The Tale of Tsar Saltan* by Rimsky-Korsakov
b10   La Traviata *(The Women Gone Astray) by Verdi*
a11   *Tosca* by Puccini
b11   Sadko *by Rimsky-Korsakov*
a12   *Tannhäuser* by Wagner
b12   L'Elisir d'Amore *(The Elixir of Love) by Donizetti*

Tie-breaker

Q   What is 'opera buffa'?
A   *Comic opera*

No. 36 Alternatives

This is a round of questions about television comics who have all been labelled (at one time or another) 'alternative'.

In *Monty Python's Flying Circus...*
a1 ...who complained about the dead parrot?
b1 ...*who was the pet shop keeper?*
a2 ...which television reporter was parodied on a desert island?
b2 ...*who created the animated cartoons?*
Which comedy groups had hits with...
a3 ...'Funky Gibbon'?
b3 ...*'The Ying-Tong Song'?*
a4 ...'I'm a Lumberjack and I'm OK'?
b4 ...*'Livin' Doll' (with Cliff Richard)?*
a5 Who starred in *Colin's Sandwich*?
b5 *Which children's author was parodied in the first* Comic Strip Presents... *show?*
a6 Who starred in her own series *Murder Most Horrid*?
b6 *With whom did she co-star in a series that began in 1987?*
a7 Who presents *Have I Got News for You*?
b7 *And who presents* Whose Line Is it Anyway?
a8 Who was once the compère of London's Comedy Store, is bald, bulky and often appears in a too-tight suit?
b8 *Who has played an utterly unscrupulous, self-seeking MP?*
a9 In which series did he play Richie Rich?
b9 *Who is both a script writer and a stand-up comic (nicknamed 'Breathless' because of the speed of his delivery)?*
a10 Who created both Stavros and a cockney called 'Loadsamoney'?
b10 *Who appeared with Rik Mayall in* The Young Ones?
a11 Who were sometimes seen on a 'trandem' (a bicycle for three)?
b11 They once appeared with a very large version of a character from a children's animated puppet series. Who was it?
a12 Which imaginary television station did Eric Idle invent?
b12 *What was the name of Michael Palin and Terry Jones' series of parodies of traditional 'boy's own' stories?*

No. 36 Answers

a1 John Cleese
b1 *Michael Palin*
a2 Alan Whicker (on 'Whicker Island')
b2 *Terry Gilliam*
a3 The Goodies
b3 *The Goons*
a4 Monty Python
b4 *The Young Ones*
a5 Mel Smith
b5 *Enid Blyton (Five Go Mad in Dorset)*
a6 Dawn French
b6 *Jennifer Saunders (French and Saunders)*
a7 Angus Deayton
b7 *Clive Anderson*
a8 Alexei Sayle
b8 *Rik Mayall (Alan B'Stard MP)*
a9 *Filthy Rich and Catflap and Bottom*
b9 *Ben Elton*
a10 Harry Enfield
b10 *Adrian Edmondson; Nigel Planer (also Christopher Ryan)*
a11 The Goodies
b11 *Dougal (from* The Magic Roundabout*)*
a12 Rutland Weekend Television
b12 Ripping Yarns

Tie-breaker

Q Which two 'new wave' comedians had a series called *S and M*?
A *Tony Slattery and Mike McShane*

No. 37 Stage Business

Which Shakespearian work was the basis for the musical...
a1 ...*West Side Story*?
b1 ...Kiss Me, Kate?
a2 ...*Catch My Soul*?
b2 ...The Boys from Syracuse?
and which Shakespearian work was the basis for the film...
a3 ...*Chimes at Midnight*?
b3 ...Forbidden Planet?
a4 ...*Throne of Blood*?
b4 ...The Rest is Silence?
a5 Whose ghost appears in *Hamlet*?
b5 *And whose ghost appears in* Julius Caesar?
a6 For what work in the theatre is Cicely Berry famous?
b6 *For what work in the theatre is Guy Woolfenden famous?*
a7 In which play or sketch does the music hall double act George and Lily have trouble with their musical director, Bert Bently?
b7 *In which musical play do we meet the army's Song and Dance Unit, South East Asia?*
a8 A play by the German writer Günter Grass *The Plebeians Rehearse the Uprising* shows a fellow German writer adapting and rehearsing a play. Which writer and which play?
b8 *The play,* Nothing On, *opens in Weston-super-Mare, then plays disastrously in two other towns. But in which real play do we watch parts of* Nothing On?
Explain these 'stage directions'–and say in which play they occur...
a9 ...'Exit, pursued by a bear'?
b9 ...'They do not move'?
a10 ...'Two Elizabethans passing the time in a place without much visible character. They are well dressed. Each of them has a leather money bag. The reason being: they are betting on the toss of a coin'?
b10 ...'A stillness falls, and there is heard only, far away...the thud of axes striking the trees'?

No. 37 Answers

a1   *Romeo and Juliet*

b1   Taming of the Shrew

a2   *Othello* (a rock opera by Jack Good, 1970)

b2   Comedy of Errors

a3   *Henry IV*

b3   The Tempest

a4   *Macbeth*–a Japanese version

b4   Hamlet–*a German version*

a5   Hamlet's father's (the murdered king's)

b5   *Julius Caesar's*

a6   As a voice coach (especially with the Royal Shakespeare Company)

b6   *As a composer (especially of incidental music for RSC productions)*

a7   *Red Peppers* by Noël Coward (in *Tonight at 8.30*)

b7   Privates on Parade *by Peter Nichols*

a8   Bertolt Brecht and *Coriolanus*

b8   Noises Off *by Michael Frayn (It is a play about a group of actors trying to perform a comedy called* Nothing On*)*

a9   Antigonus escapes (pursued by a bear), in *The Winter's Tale* by Shakespeare, just after casting the baby Perdita adrift on the seashore

b9   *Vladimir and Estragon do nothing at the end of* Waiting for Godot *by Samuel Beckett*

a10   Rosencrantz and Guildenstern at the start of Tom Stoppard's *Rosencrantz and Guildenstern Are Dead*

b10   *The stage is almost empty at the very end of Chekhov's* The Cherry Orchard. *Feers is lying on the floor but the others have left the house*

Tie-breaker

Q   Which stage play (with only one character) is about a Liverpool housewife daydreaming in her kitchen and on holiday in Greece?

A   Shirley Valentine *(by Willy Russell)*

No. 38 Kidvid

'Kidvid' is the term used by the American magazine *Variety* to mean 'children's television'–which is the subject of this round.

a1   On *The Magic Roundabout*, who said 'Time for bed'?
b1   *And what was the name of the cow?*
In *Thunderbirds*...
a2   ...what make and colour was Lady Penelope's car?
b2   *...what was her butler's name?*
a3   ...who was the leader of International Rescue?
b3   *...what was generally considered the main technical fault of the series?*
Which human originally appeared with...
a4   ...Muffin the Mule?
b4   *...Sweep?*
a5   ...Gordon the Gopher?
b5   *...Edd the Duck?*
a6   ...Mr Turnip?
b6   *...Tingha and Tucker?*
a7   Which programme began 'Here is a house; Here is a door; Windows one, two, three, four...'?
b7   *Who was the producer of* Blue Peter *from 1962 to 1988?*
a8   Who was the 'Hot Chestnut Man'?
b8   *Who played the role of Billy Bunter?*
In which series could you have seen...
a9   ...Susan Stranks, Douglas Rae and Mick Robertson?
b9   *...Christopher Trace, Lesley Judd and Leila Williams?*
a10   ...Zippy, George and Bungle?
b10   *...Fred Dinenage, Jack Hargreaves and Marion Davies?*
Who created...
a11   *...Postman Pat?*
b11   *...Trumpton?*
a12   *...The Magic Roundabout?*
b12   *...Andy Pandy?*

No. 38 Answers

a1   Zebedee
b1   *Ermintrude*
a2   Rolls-Royce, pink
b2   *Parker*
a3   Jeff Tracey (and his four sons)
b3   *You could see the puppets' strings*
a4   Annette Mills
b4   *Harry Corbett (Sweep was Sooty's friend)*
a5   Phillip Schofield
b5   *Andy Crane*
a6   Humphrey Lestocq
b6   *Jean Morton*
a7   *Play School*
b7   *Biddy Baxter*
a8   Johnny Morris
b8   *Gerald Campion*
a9   *Magpie*
b9   Blue Peter
a10   *Rainbow* (they were the puppets)
b10   How!
a11   Ivor Wood
b11   *Gordon Murray*
a12   Serge Danot (it was later adapted for British television by Eric Thompson and, later still, by Nigel Planer)
b12   *Freda Lingstrom (and Maria Bird)*

Tie-breaker

Q   Which 'family' saga or 'soap' appeared regularly on BBC Children's Television in the mid-Fifties?

A   The Appleyards *(There was a later series called* The Thompson Family*)*

No. 39 Celluloid War

Which war was featured in...

a1   ...*The Desert Rats*?

b1   ...The Birth of a Nation?

a2   ...*The Green Berets*?

b2   ...The Blue Max?

a3   ...*The Charge of the Light Brigade*?

b3   ...Platoon?

a4   ...*Fixed Bayonets* and *The Steel Helmet*?

b4   ...Paths of Glory?

In films about the Second World War...

a5   ...what is Navarone in *The Guns of Navarone*?

b5   ...*in Where Eagles Dare what was the mission of seven paratroopers in the German Alps?*

a6   ...what was the mission of *The Dirty Dozen*?

b6   ...*which theatre of war featured in They Were Expendable?*

a7   ...in which film did Michael Caine lead a team of German commandos trying to assassinate Churchill?

b7   ...*which Beatle appeared in the film How I Won the War?*

Who played...

a8   ...Patton, in the film *Patton*?

b8   ...*Rommel, in The Desert Fox?*

a9   ...Guy Gibson, in *The Dam Busters*?

b9   ...*Douglas Bader, in Reach for the Sky?*

a10   In *Oh! What a Lovely War*, which general was played by John Mills?

b10   *And who played the music hall artiste who sang 'I'll Make a Man of You'?*

a11   Who played Sergeant York, in the 1941 film about a pacifist farm boy fighting in the First World War?

b11   *Which actor (known for his Westerns) starred in The Green Berets?*

a12   Which prisoner of war movie, based on true life stories, involved escapes from Stalag Luft North?

b12   *Which 1969 film was about a group of raw recruits, fighting in Malaya?*

No. 39 Answers

a1   The Second World War (African campaign)
b1   *American Civil War*
a2   The Vietnam War
b2   *The First World War*
a3   The Crimean War
b3   *The Vietnam War*
a4   The Korean War
b4   *The First World War*
a5   A Greek island
b5   *To rescue an officer from a castle prison*
a6   To destroy a German officer's holiday resort
b6   *The war in the Pacific*
a7   *The Eagle Has Landed*
b7   *John Lennon*
a8   George C. Scott
b8   *James Mason*
a9   Richard Todd
b9   *Kenneth More*
a10   (General Sir Douglas) Haig
b10   *Maggie Smith*
a11   Gary Cooper
b11   *John Wayne*
a12   *The Great Escape*
b12   The Virgin Soldiers

Tie-breaker

Q   Which war film, set mainly in the English Channel and northern France, is said to be the most expensive black-and-white movie ever made?

A   The Longest Day

No. 40 Props

'Props' (or properties) are items used on stage (or on a film set) during the action of a play, film or television show.

Which comedian would you most likely to be imitating if you used...

a1   ...a red fez?

b1   *...an emu?*

a2   ...a black Homburg and a coat with an astrakhan collar?

b2   *...a large armchair that makes its occupant look even shorter than he is?*

In the making of which film would you need...

a3   ...radio-controlled velociraptors?

b3   *...a bicycle (with a carrier on the handlebars) that can apparently fly through the air?*

a4   ...an Ectomobile?

b4   *...a 15-foot Alien Queen?*

In which television series would you require...

a5   ...a conveyor belt and several cuddly toys?

b5   *...a telephone, a target and a crossbow?*

a6   ...a red Jaguar, registration number 248RPA?

b6   *....a ceramic hen full of cash?*

For which Shakespearian play do you need...

a7   ...an ass's head?

b7   *...a cauldron, daggers and some tree branches?*

a8   ...a skull, several rapiers and poison to be used by a 'King'?

b8   *...three caskets and a pair of scales?*

and in which other plays would you require...

a9   ...some cucumber sandwiches and a diary?

b9   *...the posh Sunday papers and an ironing board?*

a10   ...a head in a hat box?

b10   *...a full-size Thames motorcruiser and water for it to float on?*

No. 40 Answers

a1 Tommy Cooper
b1 *Rod Hull*
a2 Tony Hancock
b2 *Ronnie Corbett*
a3 *Jurassic Park*
b3 ET–The Extra-Terrestrial
a4 *Ghost Busters*
b4 Aliens
a5 *The Generation Game*
b5 The Golden Shot
a6 *Inspector Morse*
b6 Bread *(the two-piece pot hen was kept on the kitchen table)*
a7 *A Midsummer Night's Dream* (for Bottom's transformation)
b7 Macbeth *(The cauldron for the Witches; the branches to be the 'leafy screen' taken from Birnham Wood as camouflage by the English and Norwegian soldiers)*
a8 *Hamlet* (Yorick's skull; the poison is used by the Player King during the play Hamlet has performed for his mother and uncle)
b8 The Merchant of Venice *(The caskets are at Portia's house in Belmont; the scales are brought by Shylock to the trial)*
a9 *The Importance of Being Earnest* by Oscar Wilde
b9 Look Back in Anger *by John Osborne*
a10 *Night Must Fall* by Emlyn Williams
b10 Way Upstream *by Alan Ayckbourn*

Tie-breaker

Q For what sort of television show is a sofa a necessity?
A *Almost any chat show or daytime magazine and many of the more traditional situation comedies*

No. 41 Star Names

In the world of films, by what other name are (or were) the following known:

a1 Marion Michael Morrison?
b1 *Frances Ethel Gumm?*
a2 Leslie Townes Hope?
b2 *Thomas Connery?*
a3 Frank James Cooper?
b3 *Harry Lillis Crosby?*
a4 Ruth Elizabeth Davis?
b4 *Doris von Kappelhoff?*
a5 Alicia Christian Foster?
b5 *William Claude Dukenfield?*
a6 Richard Walter Jenkins?
b6 *Maurice Joseph Micklewhite?*
a7 Frederick Austerlitz?
b7 *Benjamin Kubelsky?*
a8 Julia Elizabeth Wells?
b8 *Lucille Fay Le Sueur?*
a9 Allen Stewart Konigsberg?
b9 *Melvin Kaminsky?*
a10 Maria Magdalena von Losch?
b10 *Greta Lovisa Gustafsson?*
a11 Alexander Archibald Leach?
b11 *Margarita Carmen Cansino?*
a12 Edda van Heemstra Hepburn-Ruston?
b12 *William Henry Pratt?*

No. 41 Answers

a1   John Wayne
b1   *Judy Garland*
a2   Bob Hope
b2   *Sean Connery*
a3   Gary Cooper
b3   *Bing Crosby*
a4   Bette (say: Bet) Davis
b4   *Doris Day*
a5   Jodie Foster
b5   *W. C. Fields*
a6   Richard Burton
b6   *Michael Caine*
a7   Fred Astaire
b7   *Jack Benny*
a8   Julie Andrews
b8   *Joan Crawford*
a9   Woody Allen
b9   *Mel Brooks*
a10   Marlene Dietrich
b10   *Greta Garbo*
a11   Cary Grant
b11   *Rita Hayworth*
a12   Audrey Hepburn
b12   *Boris Karloff*

Tie-breaker

Q What was Asa Yoelson's screen name?
A *Al Jolson*

No. 42 Hidden Titles–5

Within each of these dialogues are hidden the titles of eight plays. Can you spot the titles and say which dramatist wrote each group of plays?

Team A

(*An ambitious actress meets her romantic lover on a hotel balcony*)

She You'll never guess who I've just met. Those two film producers.

He Never mind them. Listen to the band. They're playing our song. Down on the plaza.

She Sweetheart, these men. You remember. We called them the Sunshine Boys.

He Darling, let's dance. Barefoot. In the park, on the beach.

She They're an odd couple. One of them said I ought to be in pictures.

He (*Despairing of getting her attention*) Sweet charity! Listen to me.

She If I'd listened to what they said, I'd be Broadway bound by now.

Team B

(*They are tourists in a foreign resort. She is bored, tetchy. He is a bit of a wimp but quite keen to please her.*)

She So we've got a whole day to fill in this dump of a town. What do you suggest?

He Well, Sybil, I don't quite know.

She You're playing for time. Make up your mind for once.

He Well, we could take in a panorama of the whole town, a view from the bridge across the harbour.

She They charge you. The price is criminal.

He That's to discourage suicides. After the...fall...well, I mean the death of a salesman, they started charging.

She That's sick. (*Getting crosser*) Talk about the misfits. You're weird.

He Well, we could go and watch the sailing. You'd like that.

She Really, I don't need you any more.

He They say one of the yachts has got a very hunky crew, Sybil.

No. 42 Answers

Team A titles
They're Playing Our Song
Plaza Suite
The Sunshine Boys
Barefoot in the Park
The Odd Couple
I Ought to be in Pictures
Sweet Charity
Broadway Bound
and the playwright is the American, Neil Simon

Team B titles
Playing for Time
A View From the Bridge
The Price
After the Fall
Death of a Salesman
The Misfits
I Don't Need You Any More
The Crucible
and the playwright is Arthur Miller

No. 43 Open the Box

On television, who presented (or presents)...
a1 ...*3–2–1*?
b1 ...Strike It Lucky?
a2 ...*Play Your Cards Right*?
b2 ...the first networked Telethon?
a3 ...*Bullseye*?
b3 ...Winner Takes All?
a4 ...*The Late, Late Breakfast Show*?
b4 ...the BBC's first Breakfast Time *programme*?
a5 ...*Countdown*?
b5 ...Busman's Holiday?
a6 ...*Crimewatch UK*?
b6 ...Question Time *(when it first started)*?

Which show featured...
a7 ...the Gotcha Oscars?
b7 ...*Sid Snott and Captain Kremmen*?
a8 ...newsreaders called Henry and Sally?
b8 ...*a mark two starship Enterprise*?
a9 ...a real-life marriage between Alex Tatham and Sue Middleton?
b9 ...*an ex-convict and a second-hand car salesman*?

a10 Which show has been presented by Bob Monkhouse, Max Bygraves and Les Dennis?
b10 *Which quiz has been presented by David Vine and David Coleman?*
a11 By what name or title was exercise lady Diana Moran known?
b11 *In what role (and show) did Miss USA Lynda Carter star?*
a12 Which show has been introduced by Michael Miles and Des O'Connor?
b12 *And which has been introduced by Jerry Desmond and Bob Monkhouse?*

No. 43 Answers

a1   Ted Rogers
b1   *Michael Barrymore*
a2   Bruce Forsyth
b2   *Michael Aspel*
a3   Jim Bowen
b3   *Jimmy Tarbuck*
a4   Noel Edmonds
b4   *Frank Bough and Selina Scott*
a5   Richard Whiteley
b5   *Julian Pettifer*
a6   Nick Ross and Sue Cook
b6   *Sir Robin Day*
a7   *Noel's Houseparty* (with Noel Edmonds)
b7   The Kenny Everett Video Show
a8   *Drop the Dead Donkey*
b8   Star Trek: the Next Generation
a9   *Blind Date* (in 1991)
b9   Minder *(originally* The Minder*)*
a10   *Family Fortunes*
b10   A Question of Sport
a11   The Green Goddess
b11   Wonder Woman
a12   *Take Your Pick*
b12   The $64,000 Question

Tie-breaker

Q   Which show or station was first presented by David Frost, Michael Parkinson, Angela Rippon, Anna Ford and Robert Kee?

A   TV-AM

No. 44 Famous for Saying...

On which television show did we regularly hear...

a1 ...'Beam me up, Scotty'?

b1 ...'Come on down'?

a2 ...'And now from Norwich...'?

b2 ...'Smile, you're on...'?

a3 ...'Seriously though, he's doing a grand job'?

b3 ...'She who must be obeyed'?

On television, who has been famous for saying...

a4 ...'Clunk, click, every trip'?

b4 ...'This play what I have wrote'?

a5 ...'Aw, don't embarrass me'?

b5 ...'Flob-a-dob' (or something similar)?

a6 ...'I'll give the results in reverse order'?

b6 ...'It's all done in the best possible taste'?

a7 ..."E's taking an early bath'?

b7 ...'Oh I say, what a supah volley'?

And on radio, who was famous for saying...

a8 ...'Hello twins'?

b8 ...'Groovy baby'?

a9 ...'Old ones, new ones'?

b9 ...'Slow, slow, quick-quick, slow'?

a10 ...'Jolly hockey sticks!'?

b10 ...'Have you ever had any embarrassing moments?'?

a11 ...'Ay thang yew'?

b11 ...'Here's to the next time'?

a12 ...'Nature's black-coated workers'?

b12 ...'Keynsham–that's K-E-Y-N-S-H-A-M'?

No. 44 Answers

a1 *Star Trek*
b1 The Price Is Right
a2 *Sale of the Century*
b2 Candid Camera
a3 *That Was The Week That Was* (David Frost)
b3 Rumpole of the Bailey(Rumpole speaking about his wife, Hilda)
a4 Jimmy Savile (in the 'wear a seat belt' campaign)
b4 *Ernie Wise*
a5 Lenny the Lion (and his ventriloquist, Terry Hall)
b5 *The Flowerpot Men*
a6 Eric Morley (on 'Miss World' contests)
b6 *Kenny Everett*
a7 Eddie Waring (Rugby League commentator, of a player being sent off)
b7 *Dan Maskell (tennis commentator)*
a8 Uncle Mac (Derek McCulloch) on *Children's Hour*
b8 *Dave Cash*
a9 Semprini (the pianist)
b9 *Victor Sylvester*
a10 Beryl Reid (originally in *Educating Archie*)
b10 *Wilfred Pickles*
a11 Arthur Askey ('I thank you') (on *Band Waggon*)
b11 *Henry Hall*
a12 The Radio Doctor (Dr Charles Hill), referring to prunes
b12 *Horace Batchelor (on Radio Luxembourg, spelling out an address)*

Tie-breaker

Q Which American news presenter always closed the CBS TV Evening News with the words 'And that's the way it is'?

A *Walter Cronkite*

No. 45 Get the Guest–3

How many clues do you need before you can identify each of the following famous actors? (See page 9)

Guest A

1 I made my first stage appearance at the Lyceum, Sunderland (in northeast England) in 1856.

2 It was in *Katharine and Petruchio* that I first appeared with Ellen Terry.

3 I was one of the last great actor-managers and the first actor to be knighted.

4 I have often been associated with 'The bells, the bells...'

Guest B

1 For several seasons, I was the leading lady at Miss Horniman's repertory company in Manchester.

2 In 1929, my brother Russell wrote my biography.

3 To celebrate our golden wedding, my husband and I appeared in *Eighty in the Shade*.

4 Down in Leatherhead in southern England, they graciously named a theatre after me.

Guest C

1 I first acted in 1888 and was once described as 'a glorious, impossible woman'.

2 It was I who said, 'It doesn't matter what you do in the bedroom as long as you don't do it in the streets and frighten the horses.'

3 My lengthy correspondence with my friend Bernard Shaw was subsequently published.

Guest D

1 Educated in Lichfield in the English Midlands, I was a pupil of the great writer, Dr Samuel Johnson.

2 I had particular success in playing the title roles in both *Macbeth* and *King Lear*.

3 Though another London theatre bears my name, my own theatre was in Drury Lane.

No. 45 Answers

Guest A Sir Henry Irving (1838–1905)
He acted with Ellen Terry for the first time in an 1867 revival of
Garrick's *Katharine and Petruchio*. *The Bells* (by Leopold Lewis) gave
Irving his first great part. It held a central place in Irving's repertoire for
the rest of his life. A knighthood was bestowed on him in 1895.

Guest B Dame (Agnes) Sybil Thorndike (1882–1976)
She joined Miss Horniman's company in 1908 after touring America in
an extraordinary wide variety of Shakespearian roles, male as well as
female. During and after the Second World War she toured widely with
the Old Vic company. In the latter part of her career she frequently
appeared with her husband, Lewis Casson. Her final performance in
1966 inaugurated a new theatre in Surrey named after her.

Guest C Mrs Patrick Campbell (1865–1940)
She became a star when she created the title role in Pinero's *The Second
Mrs Tanqueray* (1893) and also played Juliet (1896) and Ophelia (1897).
Shaw, who recognized in her a supremacy in comedy, wrote *Caesar and
Cleopatra* for her but she never performed it. Instead, nearing 50, she
created Eliza Doolittle in *Pygmalion* (1914), the last and greatest scandal
of her London career.

Guest D David Garrick (1717–1779)
Born in Hereford, he was educated at Lichfield enrolling in Dr Johnson's
school at one stage. He began acting as an amateur but his family disap-
proved and he acted under a pseudonym in Ipswich. In 1741 his performance as Richard III won him immediate success. In 1747 he signed an
agreement of partnership in the Drury Lane Theatre, inaugurating 29
years as its manager.

No. 46 Great Titles, Never Mind the Films

Can you complete the following film titles? (This might be played as a 'speed' round, seeing who can complete each title first.) (See also quiz No.96)

a1 *The Charge of the...?*
b1 *A Fish called...?*
a2 *Elmer...?*
b2 *Jailhouse...?*
a3 *The Best Little...?*
b3 *Gun Fight at the...?*
a4 *Bednobs and...?*
b4 *Chariots...?*
a5 *Bob and Carol...?*
b5 *Alice Doesn't...?*
a6 *Carleton-Browne of...?*
b6 *Dr Strangelove, or...?*
a7 *Everything You Always Wanted...?*
b7 *The Amityville...?*
a8 *All Quiet on...?*
b8 *Ice Cold...?*
a9 *Desperately Seeking...?*
b9 *Hannah and...?*
a10 *Born on the...?*
b10 *For a Few...?*
a11 *Every Which Way...?*
b11 *Has Anybody...?*
a12 *The Heart Is...?*
b12 *Fahrenheit...?*

No. 46 Answers

a1 *Light Brigade*
b1 Wanda
a2 *Gantry*
b2 Rock
a3 *Whorehouse in Texas*
b3 OK Corral
a4 *Broomsticks*
b4 of Fire
a5 *and Ted and Alice*
b5 Live Here Anymore
a6 *the FO* (Foreign Office)
b6 How I Learned to Stop Worrying and Love the Bomb
a7 *to Know About Sex But Were Afraid to Ask*
b7 Horror
a8 *the Western Front*
b8 in Alex
a9 *Susan*
b9 Her Sisters
a10 *Fourth of July*
b10 Dollars More
a11 *But Loose*
b11 Seen My Gal?
a12 *a Lonely Hunter*
b12 451

Tie-breaker

Q Which films can you think of whose title begins with the word 'Blue'?

A Blue, Blue Blood, Blue Collar, Blue Denim, Blue Hawaii, Blue Murder at St Trinians, Blue Skies, Blue Thunder, Blue Velvet, Blue Water White Death.

No. 47 Songs from the Shows–2

In which musical does each of the following numbers occur:

a1 'On the Street Where You Live'?

b1 *'The Farmer and the Cowman'?*

a2 'We Said We Wouldn't Look Back?

b2 *'Matchmaker, Matchmaker'?*

a3 'Some Enchanted Evening'?

b3 *'Good Morning, Starshine'?*

a4 'Day by Day'?

b4 *'Climb Every Mountain'?*

a5 'I Could Be Happy With You'?

b5 *'Shall We Dance, Shall We Dance?'?*

a6 'One'?

b6 *'Flash! Bang! Wallop!'?*

a7 'Luck Be a Lady'?

b7 *'Gee, Officer Krupke'?*

a8 'You've Got to Pick a Pocket or Two'?

b8 *'If You Could See Her Through My Eyes'?*

a9 'There's No Business Like Show Business'?

b9 *'Another Opening, Another Show'?*

a10 'Don't Cry for Me, Argentina'?

b10 *'I Could Write a Book'?*

a11 'I Love Paris'?

b11 *'June is Bustin' Out All Over'?*

a12 'I Talk to the Trees'?

b12 *'Hernando's Hideaway'?*

No. 47 Answers

a1 *My Fair Lady*
b1 Oklahoma!
a2 *Salad Days*
b2 Fiddler on the Roof
a3 *South Pacific*
b3 Hair
a4 *Godspell*
b4 The Sound of Music
a5 *The Boy Friend*
b5 The King and I
a6 *A Chorus Line*
b6 Half a Sixpence
a7 *Guys and Dolls*
b7 West Side Story
a8 *Oliver!*
b8 Cabaret
a9 *Annie Get Your Gun*
b9 Kiss Me, Kate
a10 *Evita*
b10 Pal Joey
a11 *Can Can*
b11 Carousel
a12 *Paint Your Wagon*
b12 The Pajama Game

Tie-breaker

Q From which film musical come the songs 'The Roses of Success', 'Truly Scrumptious' and 'Hushabye Mountain'?
A Chitty Chitty Bang Bang

No. 48 On Location

Which television series was (or is) set in each of these fictional locations:

a1 Ramsey Street?
b1 *Beckindale?*
a2 Walford?
b2 *Weatherfield?*
a3 Southfork?
b3 *Wentworth?*
a4 Grantley Manor?
b4 *East Cheam?*
a5 Slade Prison?
b5 *Maplin's?*
a6 Crinkly Bottom?
b6 *Newtown?*
a7 Holby?
b7 *Oxbridge Hospital?*
a8 St Angela's Hospital?
b8 *Blair Hospital?*
a9 Glendarroch?
b9 *Tannochbrae?*
a10 Tarrant?
b10 *Walmington on Sea?*
a11 Shilo Ranch?
b11 *Wameru?*
a12 Angleton?
b12 *Sullbridge?*

No. 48 Answers

a1 *Neighbours*
b1 Emmerdale Farm
a2 *EastEnders*
b2 Coronation Street
a3 *Dallas*
b3 Cell Block H *(Wentworth Detention Centre)*
a4 *To the Manor Born*
b4 Hancock's Half Hour
a5 *Porridge*
b5 Hi-de-Hi!
a6 *Noel's Houseparty*
b6 Z-Cars
a7 *Casualty*
b7 Emergency–Ward 10
a8 *Angels*
b8 Dr Kildare
a9 *Take the High Road*
b9 Dr Finlay's Casebook
a10 *Howard's Way*
b10 Dad's Army
a11 *The Virginian*
b11 Daktari *(Wameru Study Centre)*
a12 *The Newcomers*
b12 Starr and Company

Tie-breaker

Q Which real house was used as Brideshead in the television series *Brideshead Revisited*?

A *Castle Howard*

No. 49 The Western

In the cinema...

a1 In which film did John Wayne play cavalry officer Nathan Brittles?

b1 And whom did he play in The Alamo?

a2 Who played Marshall Will Kane in *High Noon*?

b2 Who produced the film?

a3 Which famous 1939 film tells of a group of characters travelling West–and under attack from Indians?

b3 Who played the Ringo Kid in that film?

a4 In the same film, who played the 'whore with a heart of gold'?

b4 Who directed the film?

a5 Which 1956 film by the same director has the same star, this time hunting for his niece?

b5 What had happened to her?

On television...

a6 ...which cowboy series (about cattle driving in Kansas) starred Clint Eastwood?

b6 ...which one was the story of the Cartwright family?

a7 ...which cowboy series saw Ty Hardin cleaning up the West?

b7 ...and which series had Burt Reynolds as the leader of a group of cowboys on the River Mississippi?

Film or TV...

a8 In which Western did Major Adams lead pioneers westwards?

b8 Which rather small actor played the mysterious stranger in Shane?

a9 Who played Doc Holliday in *Gunfight at the OK Corral*?

b9 Who played Wyatt Earp in that film?

a10 Who played him in *My Darling Clementine*?

b10 And who played him in Cheyenne Autumn?

a11 Who played General Custer in *Custer of the West*?

b11 And who played him in They Died with Their Boots On?

a12 What was notable about the 1903 film *The Great Train Robbery*?

b12 Which American film was based on the Japanese Seven Samurai?

No. 49 Answers

a1 *She Wore a Yellow Ribbon*
b1 *Davy Crockett*
a2 Gary Cooper
b2 *Stanley Kramer*
a3 *Stagecoach*
b3 *John Wayne*
a4 Claire Trevor
b4 *John Ford*
a5 *The Searchers*
b5 *She'd been kidnapped and brought up by Indians (by a Comanche chief)*
a6 *Rawhide*
b6 Bonanza
a7 *Bronco*
b7 Riverboat
a8 *Wagon Train*
b8 Alan Ladd
a9 Kirk Douglas
b9 *Burt Lancaster*
a10 Henry Fonda
b10 *James Stewart*
a11 Robert Shaw
b11 *Errol Flynn*
a12 It is generally accepted as the first 'Western'; also the first film to tell a story
b12 The Magnificent Seven

Tie-breaker

Q Can you name the actors who played the 'Seven'?
A *Yul Brynner, Steve McQueen, Robert Vaughn, Charles Bronson, Horst Buchholz, Brad Dexter and James Coburn*

No. 50 Dramatis Personae–2

In which play do the following characters appear–and who wrote each play?

a1   Riff Raff and Frank 'N' Furter?
b1   *Archie Rice?*
a2   Robert Browning and Elizabeth Barrett Moulton-Barrett?
b2   *A wrestler called Charles?*
a3   Giles and Mollie Ralston and Detective Sergeant Trotter?
b3   *King Creon?*
a4   Enobarbus?
b4   *Hamm, Clov, Nagg and Nell?*
a5   Sir Jasper Fidget and Mrs Margery Pinchwife?
b5   *Willy Loman?*
a6   Peter Dobchinsky and Peter Bobchinsky?
b6   *Inspector Truscott?*
a7   Mistress Ford and Mistress Page?
b7   *Lady Undershaft and Barbara Undershaft?*
a8   Mean old Harpagon?
b8   *Ex-convict Jean Valjean?*
a9   Tobias Rigg, Mrs Lovett and her pies?
b9   *Sir Robert Morton and Ronnie?*
a10   The mother, the bride, Leonardo and the wife of Leonardo?
b10   *Christy Mahon?*
a11   Madame Arcati?
b11   *Andrew and Millie Crocker-Harris?*
a12   Trofimov, Feers and Yasha?
b12   *Halvard Solness*

No. 50 Answers

a1 *The Rocky Horror Show* by Richard O'Brien
b1 The Entertainer *by John Osborne*
a2 *The Barretts of Wimpole Street* by Rudolph Bessier
b2 As You Like It *by William Shakespeare*
a3 *The Mousetrap* by Agatha Christie
b3 Antigone *(in the plays by Sophocles and Jean Anouilh)*
a4 *Antony and Cleopatra* by William Shakespeare
b4 Endgame *by Samuel Beckett*
a5 *The Country Wife* by William Wycherley
b5 Death of a Salesman *by Arthur Miller*
a6 *The Government Inspector* by Nikolai Gogol
b6 Loot *by Joe Orton*
a7 *The Merry Wives of Windsor* by William Shakespeare
b7 Major Barbara *by Bernard Shaw*
a8 *The Miser (L'Avare)* by Moliere
b8 Les Miserables *by Alain Boublil, Claude-Michel Schönberg, Herbert Kretzmer and James Fenton*
a9 *Sweeney Todd* (including one by Christopher Bond, based on a story by George Dibdin Pitt; also the Sondheim/Wheeler musical)
b9 The Winslow Boy *by Terence Rattigan*
a10 *Blood Wedding* by Federico Garcia Lorca
b10 The Playboy of the Western World *by J. M. Synge*
a11 *Blithe Spirit* by Noël Coward
b11 The Browning Version *by Terence Rattigan*
a12 *The Cherry Orchard* by Anton Chekhov
b12 The Master Builder *by Henrik Ibsen*

Tie-breaker

Q Which of Eugene O'Neill's plays is about the Tyrone family and their attempts to cope with drug addiction and alcoholism?

A Long Day's Journey into Night

No. 51 Best Actresses

Who won an Oscar for Best Actress with the following films:

a1 *Who's Afraid of Virginia Woolf?* (1966)?
b1 Cabaret *(1972)?*
a2 *The Prime of Miss Jean Brodie* (1969)?
b2 Mary Poppins *(1964)?*
a3 *Women in Love* (1970)?
b3 Terms of Endearment *(1983)?*
a4 *Darling* (1965)?
b4 Moonstruck *(1987)?*
a5 *The Accused* (1988)?
b5 A Streetcar Named Desire *(1951)?*
a6 *Annie Hall* (1977)?
b6 Coming Home *(1978)?*
a7 *Gaslight* (1944)?
b7 Roman Holiday *(1953)?*
a8 *Room at the Top* (1959)?
b8 Jezebel *(1938)?*
a9 *Driving Miss Daisy* (1989)?
b9 Mrs Miniver *(1942)?*
a10 *Born Yesterday* (1950)?
b10 The Miracle Worker *(1962)?*
a11 *Sophie's Choice* (1982)?
b11 To Each His Own *(1946)?*
a12 *Children of a Lesser God* (1986)?
b12 Coquette *(1928–29)?*

No. 51 Answers

a1	Elizabeth Taylor
b1	*Liza Minnelli*
a2	Maggie Smith
b2	*Julie Andrews*
a3	Glenda Jackson
b3	*Shirley MacLaine*
a4	Julie Christie
b4	*Cher*
a5	Jodie Foster
b5	*Vivien Leigh*
a6	Diane Keaton
b6	*Jane Fonda*
a7	Ingrid Bergman
b7	*Audrey Hepburn*
a8	Simone Signoret
b8	*Bette Davis*
a9	Jessica Tandy
b9	*Greer Garson*
a10	Judy Holliday
b10	*Anne Bancroft*
a11	Meryl Streep
b11	*Olivia de Havilland*
a12	Marlee Matlin
b12	*Mary Pickford*

Tie-breaker

Q For which season's films were Oscars first awarded: was it 1920–21, 1927–28 or 1928–29?

A *1927–1928 (From 1934 they were awarded for the calendar year)*

No. 52 Hidden Titles–6

Within each of these dialogues are hidden eight film titles. Can you spot the titles–and also say which personality links each group of films?

Team A
(*The scene is a New York casino. Both characters are a little drunk*)

She You know, this is the best casino in Manhattan.

He This casino's royal. Just don't drink the water, Annie.

She Where's the barman?

He Gone. I told him to go. Take the money and run, I said.

She (*Giggles*) You're drunk, Sam.

He So what's new, pussy?

She Cat! I'm going to take you home.

He Why?

She (*Whispered giggle*) To tell you everything you always wanted to know.

He About sex?

She Shhh.

He (*Flattering her*) Annie Hall, you're an amazing woman.

She Still playing the same tune?

He So?

She I don't care if you do play it again, Sam.

Team B
(*He is a suspicious lover; she is a young innocent*)

He So you know this man well? How did you meet?

She We're complete strangers. (*Pause*) On a train, if you must know.

He Where were you going?

She Up north. By North Western Railway.

He And he got in your carriage?

She There was a window open. A rear window–

He So?

She I was trying to fix a torn curtain to stop the draught and he had some rope.

He You speak to weird men who happen to have a length of rope in their brief cases?

She Now don't go getting in a frenzy–

He So because you pick up a complete stranger, I must be a psy-chopath?

She I've only got to talk to another man and in your imagination you dial M for murder.

No. 52 Answers

Team A titles

Manhattan (actor, writer, director)

Casino Royale (actor, co-writer)

Don't Drink the Water (writer)

Take the Money and Run (actor, writer, director)

What's New Pussy Cat? (actor, director)

Everything You Always Wanted to Know About Sex (actor, writer, producer, director)

Annie Hall (actor, co-writer, director)

Play It Again Sam (actor, writer)

and the personality is Woody Allen–who was writer, director, producer and an actor in the films, as shown

Team B titles

Strangers on a Train

North by North-West

Rear Window

Torn Curtain

Rope

Frenzy

Psycho

Dial M for Murder

and the personality is the director of all eight films, Alfred Hitchcock

No. 53 Soap on the Box–1

a1 In *Dallas*, who originally played Miss Ellie?
b1 *Who took over the role in 1984?*
a2 What was the name of her first husband?
b2 *And who was her second husband?*

and in other soaps, who were these man-eaters?
a3 ...She said 'I do' to both Arnold *and* Steve Tanner
b3 ...'Prim, prissy and sweet', she burned not in hell but in a car crash
a4 ...Joan Collins played this 'super bitch' who loathes Krystle
b4 ...She lost Jason but teamed up with Zac

and who were these old gossips?
a5 ...A bit of a fortune-teller and fond of her pug
b5 ...Her husband Len was usually missing, perhaps because she was such a sourpuss
a6 ...Always in haircurlers, she lived at No. 13
b6 ...A charlady who was once accused of being a Russian spy

In which soap did...
a7 ...Trish Valentine have a troublesome toyboy?
b7 ...Eddie the Landlord get bumped off?
a8 ...Sue Sullivan and baby Daniel get killed?
b8 ...and 'Who dunnit'?

In which soap did...
a9 ...Tom and Pippa Fletcher move to Summer Bay?
b9 ...Mark Greenstreet get involved with horses?
a10 ...Jill Chance finally choose John Maddingham?
b10 ...Lynne love the 'Flying Fish' and fall into the harbour?
a11 ...Mike Thompson leave Cheshire for Sydney, Australia?
b11 ...Damon and Debbie go off to appear in their own series?
a12 ...in *Crossroads*, whom did Meg Richardson marry in 1975?
b12 ...who played the chauffeur of their honeymoon Rolls-Royce?

No. 53 Answers

a1 Barbara Bel Geddes
b1 *Donna Reed*
a2 Jock
b2 *Clayton Farlow*
a3 Elsie Tanner in *Coronation Street*
b3 *Pamela Ewing in* Dallas
a4 Alexis Rowan (or Carrington, Colby, Dexter, etc!) in *Dynasty*
b4 *Sable Colby in* The Colbys
a5 Ethel Skinner in *EastEnders*
b5 *Nell Mangel in* Neighbours
a6 Hilda Ogden in *Coronation Street*
b6 *Amy Turtle in* Crossroads
a7 *Eldorado*
b7 EastEnders *(the landlord of the Queen Vic)*
a8 *Brookside*
b8 *Barry Grant (a former lover)*
a9 *Home and Away*
b9 Trainer
a10 *Crossroads* (in the very last episode)
b10 Howard's Way
a11 *Families*
b11 Brookside *(the characters appeared in a three-part 'spin off' series called* Damon and Debbie*)*
a12 Hugh Mortimer
b12 *Larry Grayson*

Tie-breaker

Q Which was the first Australian soap opera broadcast on British television?

A The Sullivans

No. 54 Quote...Unquote

In which radio programmes did the following sayings originate–and become 'catch phrases'?

a1 'Give 'im the money, Barney!'?
b1 'And the next object is...'?
a2 'I don't mind if I do'?
b2 'He's fallen in the water'?
a3 'The time in Britain is 12 noon; in Germany it's one o'clock–at home and away it's time for...'?
b3 'Without deviation, hesitation or repetition'?
a4 'Left hand down a bit'?
b4 'We stop the roar of London's traffic'?
a5 'It's disgraceful, it ought not to be allowed'?
b5 'Are you sitting comfortably'?
a6 'The answer lies in the soil'?
b6 'I've arrived and to prove it I'm here'?
a7 'I'm worried about Jim'?
b7 'Oooo arr, me ol' pal, me ol' beauty'?
a8 'A mauve one!'?
b8 'Good morning, sir, was there something?'?
a9 'It all depends what you mean by...'?
b9 'The legal eagle'?
a10 'He's lovely, Mrs Hoskin, he's lovely'?
b10 'Steady, Barker'?
a11 'Apart from the Bible and Shakespeare'?
b11 'Don't miss the next episode of...'?
a12 'Doesn't it make you want to spit!'?
b12 'What me–in my state of health?'?

No. 54 Answers

a1 *Have A Go* (said by Wilfred Pickles to the show's producer, Barney Colehan)

b1 Twenty Questions

a2 *ITMA* (*It's That Man Again*) (spoken by Jack Train, as Colonel Chinstrap)

b2 The Goon Show

a3 *Two-Way Family Favourites*

b3 Just A Minute

a4 *The Navy Lark* (said by Leslie Phillips)

b4 In Town Tonight

a5 *Children's Hour*: 'Toytown' (spoken by 'Mr Growser')

b5 Listen With Mother *(Julia Lang, originally)*

a6 *Beyond Our Ken* (Kenneth Williams)

b6 Educating Archie *(Max Bygraves)*

a7 *Mrs Dale's Diary* and/or *The Dales*

b7 The Archers *(Walter Gabriel, played by Chris Gittins)*

a8 *Take It From Here* (Jimmy Edwards)

b8 Much Binding-in-the-Marsh *(Sam Costa)*

a9 *The Brains Trust* (Professor Joad's regular answer)

b9 The Jimmy Young Show *(referring to his legal expert)*

a10 *Ray's A Laugh* (Ted Ray)

b10 Just Fancy; *also* Merry-Go-Round *(both starring Eric Barker)*

a11 *Desert Island Discs*

b11 Dick Barton–Special Agent!

a12 *Band Waggon* (Arthur Askey)

b12 ITMA *(It's That Man Again) (spoken by Fred Yule as Charles Atlas)*

Tie-breaker

Q Which pre-Second World War (and post-war) show originated the phrase 'This week's deliberate mistake'?

A Monday Night At Seven *(later,* Monday Night At Eight) *in a regular spot called 'Puzzle Corner'*

No. 55 G and S

The keenest fans of Gilbert and Sullivan have no trouble reciting (or singing) Gilbert's lyrics by heart–but how well do you know them? Can you fill in the gaps and say from which opera each of these quotations comes?

1 'I am the very ...(a)... of a modern ...(b)...'
2 'She may very well pass for ...(a)...
  In the dusk with a ...(b)...!'
3 ' "Is it weakness of intellect, birdie?" I cried,
  "Or a ...(a)... in your ...(b)..."
  With a shake of his poor little head he replied,"...(c)...!" '
4 'And I'm never, never ...(a)...
  What, never?
  No, never!
  What, *never*?
  Hardly ever!
  He's hardly ever ...(a)...
  Then give ...(b)..., and one cheer more
  For the ...(c)...!'
5 'I often think it's comical
  How Nature always does contrive
  That ...(a)...
  That's born into the world alive,
  Is either ...(b)...
  Or ...(c)...'
6 'As some day it may happen that a victim must be found,
  I've ...(a)...
  Of ...(b)... who might well be
  underground,
  and ...(c)...'

No. 55 Answers

1 (a) model
   (b) Major-General
   from *Pirates of Penzance*
2 (a) 43
   (b) light behind her!
   from *Trial by Jury*
3 (a) rather tough worm
   (b) little inside?
   (c) Oh, willow, titwillow, titwillow!
   from *The Mikado*
4 (a) sick at sea!
   (b) three cheers
   (c) hardy Captain of the 'Pinafore'!
   from *HMS Pinafore*
5 (a) every boy and every gal
   (b) a little Liberal
   (c) else a little Conservative!
   from *Iolanthe*
6 (a) got a little list–I've got a little list
   (b) society offenders
   (c) who never would be missed–who never would be missed
   from *The Mikado*

Tie-breaker

Q Gilbert once complained an actor never got his words right.
'But,' said the actor, 'I know my lines.' What did Gilbert reply?

A *'That may be, but you don't know mine'*

No. 56 Animals on Screen

What kind of creature was...
a1   ...Flipper?
b1   ...*Rin Tin Tin*?
a2   ...Cheta?
b2   ...*Trigger*?
a3   ...Clarence?
b3   ...*Roobarb*?

Whose pet, 'assistant' or 'friend' was...
a4   ...Snowy the dog?
b4   ...*Simba the lion*?
a5   ...Pedro the bloodhound?
b5   ...*Judy the chimp*?
a6   Who was Petra?
b6   *And on the same show, who was Lulu?*
a7   Whose dog was Shep?
b7   *And in which series did the teddy bear Aloysius feature?*
a8   Which 'animal' has partnered Derek Fowlds?
b8   *And who partnered Fay Wray?*
a9   Which animal is featured in the films (all sequels) *The Hills of Home, The Sun Comes Up* and *The Painted Hills*?
b9   *Which was the first film in the series?*

Which is the missing creature from these film titles...
a10   ...*Dundee*?
b10   ...*Ballou*?
a11   *The...Hunter*?
b11   *The Day of the...?*
a12   *The Flight of the...?*
b12   *Dear...?*

No. 56 Answers

a1   A dolphin
b1   *A dog*
a2   A chimpanzee (in the Tarzan films)
b2   *A horse (Roy Rogers')*
a3   A lion ('the cross-eyed lion')
b3   *A cat*
a4   Tintin
b4   *Jungle Boy*
a5   Sexton Blake
b5   *Dr Marsh Tracy*
a6   The pet alsatian in *Blue Peter*
b6   *The baby elephant that 'misbehaved' on camera*
a7   John Noakes
b7   *Brideshead Revisited*
a8   Basil Brush
b8   *King Kong*
a9   Lassie
b9   *Lassie Come Home*
a10   *Crocodile*
b10   Cat
a11   *Deer*
b11   Jackal *or* Locust
a12   *Phoenix or Doves*
b12   Octopus

Tie-breaker

Q   What was the name of the dog in the 'Blondie' series of films (about Dagwood Bumstead and his wife, Blondie)?
A   *Daisy*

No. 57 If It's Act One, It Must Be...

Which country is the setting of...

a1 ...the musical, *Cabaret*?

b1 ...*the musical,* Can Can*?*

a2 ...the play *A View from the Bridge* (by Arthur Miller)?

b2 ...*the comic opera* The Mikado *(by Gilbert and Sullivan)?*

a3 ...the play *Juno and the Paycock* (by Sean O'Casey)?

b3 ...*the farce* Accidental Death of an Anarchist *(by Dario Fo)?*

and which play is set in...

a4 ...Sicilia and Bohemia?

b4 ...*Spain and Peru?*

a5 ...a jungle and Rome?

b5 ...*Venice and Cyprus?*

a6 ...London and Strelsau?

b6 ...*Llareggub?*

a7 ...Moscow and a posh London tailor's?

b7 ...*Jummapur, India and Shepperton, Surrey?*

and which countries are the settings for...

a8 ...Shakespeare's *Antony and Cleopatra*?

b8 ...*Marlowe's* Doctor Faustus*?*

a9 Which two countries feature in Chekhov's *The Cherry Orchard*?

b9 *And with which two countries might Bertolt Brecht's The Resistible Rise of Arturo Ui be said to be associated?*

a10 In which country does Pieter-Dirk Uys regularly set his plays–plays such as *Paradise is Closing Down* and *God's Forgotten*?

b10 *And which country is the setting of Michael Hastings' 1977 play about despotism and tyranny,* For the West*?*

No. 57 Answers

a1 Germany (Berlin)

b1 *France (Paris)*

a2 United States of America (Brooklyn, New York)

b2 *Japan (the imaginary town of Titipu)*

a3 Ireland (Dublin)

b3 *Italy*

a4 *The Winter's Tale* by Shakespeare

b4 The Royal Hunt of the Sun *by Peter Shaffer*

a5 *Androcles and the Lion* by Bernard Shaw

b5 Othello *by Shakespeare*

a6 *Prisoner of Zenda* (the novel by Anthony Hope adapted for the stage by various dramatizers e.g. Matthew Francis)

b6 Under Milk Wood *by Dylan Thomas*

a7 *An Englishman Abroad* by Alan Bennett (within the double bill *Single Spies*)

b7 In the Native State *by Tom Stoppard*

a8 Egypt (Alexandria), Sicily (Messina), Syria ('A Plain') and Greece (Athens and Actium)

b8 *Germany (Wittenberg) and 'Italy' (The Vatican), and also his reported travels took him to Germany (Trier), France (Paris), Naples, Venice and Padua. (Italy did not technically exist as one country at that time. For 'Germany' accept: Holy Roman Empire)*

a9 Russia (where it is set) and France (where Mme Ranevsky (the owner of the orchard) has been living

b9 *United States of America (it is set in Chicago) but it is also a satire on Nazism and Hitler–hence Germany*

a10 South Africa (they're both set in Cape Town)

b10 *Uganda*

Tie-breaker

Q Which Shakespreare play was the first production of the National Theatre?

A Hamlet

No. 58 Jobs for the Boys (and Girls)

The credits at the end of a film or television programme sometimes look as if they include everyone who has come within three miles of the show–plus the director's auntie. How many of these job descriptions can you explain?

a1 Director?
b1 *Producer?*
a2 Production assistant?
b2 *Clapperboy?*
a3 Stagehand?
b3 *Designer?*
a4 Dresser?
b4 *Sparks?*
a5 Bit part?
b5 *Walk-on?*
a6 Technical supervisor?
b6 *Lighting supervisor?*
a7 Buyer?
b7 *Lighting cameraman?*
a8 Film editor?
b8 *Floor manager?*
a9 Gaffer?
b9 *Dubbing mixer?*
a10 Grip?
b10 *Unit manager?*
a11 Executive producer?
b11 *Associate producer?*
a12 Rostrum cameraman?
b12 *Vision mixer?*

No. 58 Answers

a1 The person immediately in charge of a programme, who is directly responsible for getting it onto the screen or on to video tape or film

b1 *The individual who exercises control over all aspects of a production, especially the financial side*

a2 A director's personal assistant

b2 *The camera assistant who operates the clapperboard*

a3 Member of the studio floor crew who rigs and clears the sets

b3 *The person responsible for the look of the sets in a programme*

a4 A wardrobe assistant engaged to help in costume changes

b4 *An electrician*

a5 A small role in a play or film

b5 *An 'extra' who is asked to perform a definite function and attracts additional payment (e.g. 'Man with dog'; 'Woman in launderette')*

a6 A senior technician overseeing all technical output of a studio

b6 *The senior technician in charge of all lighting in a studio*

a7 A member of the property department who has to hire or buy items of furniture, etc. for a programme

b7 *The leading cameraman of a film unit who is responsible not only for the film image but also for the lighting*

a8 The technician responsible for cutting and shaping film sequences

b8 *The technician who is responsible to the director for cueing the cast and for general discipline during transmission or recording*

a9 A chief electrician

b9 *The technician responsible for blending speech, music, incidental sound and sound effects on a film or videotape*

a10 A person who serves a film crew (often by laying tracks on which a mobile camera can be moved)

b10 *In filming, the person responsible for catering, travel arrangements, etc.*

a11 The person in overall charge of a programme department

b11 *An assistant to a producer who has no clearly defined job*

a12 A person who operates a film camera, positioned directly above a table, which takes stills or close-ups

b12 *Control-room operator who switches from one camera to another*

No. 59 Sci Fi in the Cinema

Which film is associated with the slogan...

a1 ...'Phone home'?

b1 ...'You'll believe a man can fly'?

a2 ...'May the Force be with you'?

b2 ...'In Space, no one can hear you scream'?

a3 Who was Superman in the 1978 *Superman*?

b3 And which role was played by Margot Kidder?

a4 Who was the 'prehistoric' pin-up in *One Million Years* BC?

b4 In which film was she miniaturized and injected into a man's body to perform brain surgery?

a5 Who played Luke Skywalker in *Star Wars*?

b5 And who played Ben Kenobi?

a6 Which film, set in Los Angeles in 2019 AD, features Harrison Ford and Sean Young?

b6 In which 1987 film was Peter Weller half-human, half-machine?

a7 Who was the star of *Total Recall*?

b7 In which film does an eccentric scientist help a teenager to travel to the Fifties to meet his parents?

a8 Which 1990 film was about a lover who dies and comes back to Earth to protect his girlfriend?

b8 Who played the girlfriend?

a9 Which space fiction film opened with an army of monkeys on horseback?

b9 Who was its star?

a10 Which 1936 film began with a world war and ended with man's first space flight?

b10 Who wrote the novel on which it was based?

a11 Who played the suburban power-worker whose life was changed by *Close Encounters of the Third Kind*?

b11 Which French film maker had a role in the film?

a12 In which 1964 film did a Victorian space craft visit the Moon?

b12 And in which 1963 film did a tiny duchy send a rocket propelled by wine to the Moon?

No. 59 Answers

a1 *ET–The Extra-Terrestrial*
b1 Superman *(1978)*
a2 *Star Wars*
b2 Alien
a3 Christopher Reeve
b3 *Lois Lane*
a4 Raquel Welch
b4 Fantastic Voyage
a5 Mark Hamill
b5 *Alec Guinness*
a6 *Blade Runner*
b6 Robocop
a7 Arnold Schwarzenegger
b7 Back to the Future
a8 *Ghost*
b8 *Demi Moore*
a9 *Planet of the Apes*
b9 *Charlton Heston*
a10 *Things to Come*
b10 *H. G. Wells* (The Shape of Things to Come*)*
a11 Richard Dreyfuss
b11 *(François) Truffaut*
a12 *The First Men in the Moon*
b12 The Mouse on the Moon

Tie-breaker

Q In 1926, a German film maker (Fritz Lang) made an epic science fiction film which involved a mad scientist, a female robot and a city almost destroyed when its slave workers revolt. What is it called?

A Metropolis

No. 60 Brush Up Your Shakespeare

From which Shakespeare play does each of these quotations come—and which character speaks each line?

a1   'Get thee to a nunnery'
b1   *'Now all the youth of England are on fire...'*
a2   'Parting is such sweet sorrow...'
b2   *'So are they all, honourable men'*
a3   'Shall there be no more cakes and ale?'
b3   *'Look in the almanac, find out moonshine!'*
a4   'Blow, winds and crack your cheeks...'
b4   *'Full fathom five thy father lies...'*
a5   'Comparisons are odorous'
b5   *'Something is rotten in the state of Denmark'*
a6   'Let's to billiards'
b6   *'They have their exits and their entrances...'*
a7   'He hath eaten me out of house and home...'
b7   *'The bell invites me...'*
a8   'O sweet Anne Page...'
b8   *'This royal throne of kings, this sceptred isle...'*
a9   'Kiss me, Kate'
b9   *'A snapper-up of unconsidered trifles...'*
a10   'A horse, a horse, my kingdom for a horse...'
b10   *'I have done the state some service...'*
a11   'This day is called the feast of Crispian...'
b11   *'If you prick us, do we not bleed?'*
a12   'A plague o' both your houses!'
b12   *'Under the greenwood tree*
        Who loves to lie with me...'

No. 60 Answers

a1   Hamlet in *Hamlet*

b1   *Chorus in* Henry V

a2   Juliet in *Romeo and Juliet*

b2   *Mark Anthony in* Julius Caesar

a3   Sir Toby Belch in *Twelfth Night*

b3   *Bottom in* A Midsummer Night's Dream

a4   Lear in *King Lear*

b4   *Ariel in* The Tempest

a5   Dogberry in *Much Ado About Nothing*

b5   *Marcellus in* Hamlet

a6   Cleopatra in *Antony and Cleopatra*

b6   *Jacques in* As You Like It

a7   Hostess (about Falstaff) in *Henry IV* Part One

b7   *Macbeth in* Macbeth

a8   Slender in *The Merry Wives of Windsor*

b8   *John of Gaunt in* Richard II

a9   Petruchio in *The Taming of the Shrew*

b9   *Autolycus in* The Winter's Tale

a10   Richard in *Richard III*

b10   *Othello in* Othello

a11   Henry V in *Henry V*

b11   *Shylock in* The Merchant of Venice

a12   Mercutio in *Romeo and Juliet*

b12   *Amiens (a Lord) in* As You Like It

Tie-breaker

Q   Which twentieth-century poet wrote:
'O O O O that Shakespeherian Rag–
It's so elegant
So intelligent...'?

A   *T. S. Eliot*

No. 61 Stars of the Sixties

Can you complete this cast list by saying who played each of these roles in famous films of the Sixties?

a1   Henry Higgins in *My Fair Lady*?
b1   Alfie in *Alfie*?
a2   The motel owner's victim in *Psycho*?
b2   James Bond's girlfriend in *Dr No*?
a3   Mark Antony in *Cleopatra*?
b3   Napoleon in *Waterloo*?
a4   Captain Bligh in the 1963 *Mutiny on the Bounty*?
b4   Fletcher Christian in the same film?
a5   Barbarella in *Barbarella*?
b5   Spartacus in *Spartacus*?
a6   Jean Brodie in *The Prime of Miss Jean Brodie*?
b6   Mrs Robinson in *The Graduate*?
a7   Humbert Humbert whose eye is caught by Lolita in *Lolita*?
b7   The pregnant wife in *Rosemary's Baby*?
a8   Billy in *Billy Liar*?
b8   Mr Chips in *Goodbye Mr Chips (1969 version)*?
a9   Charley Bubbles in *Charley Bubbles*?
b9   Sherif Ali in *Lawrence of Arabia*?
a10 Crown in *The Thomas Crown Affair*?
b10 'Sir James' in *Casino Royale*?
a11 Gudrun in *Women in Love*?
b11 Bathsheba in *Far from the Madding Crowd*?
a12 Archie Rice in *The Entertainer*?
b12 The Servant in *The Servant*?

No. 61 Answers

a1 Rex Harrison
b1 *Michael Caine*
a2 Janet Leigh
b2 *Ursula Andress*
a3 Richard Burton
b3 *Rod Steiger*
a4 Trevor Howard
b4 *Marlon Brando*
a5 Jane Fonda
b5 *Kirk Douglas*
a6 Maggie Smith
b6 *Anne Bancroft*
a7 James Mason
b7 *Mia Farrow*
a8 Tom Courtenay
b8 *Peter O'Toole*
a9 Albert Finney
b9 *Omar Sharif*
a10 Steve McQueen
b10 *David Niven*
a11 Glenda Jackson
b11 *Julie Christie*
a12 Laurence Olivier
b12 *Dirk Bogarde*

Tie-breaker

Q Who played Bonnie Parker and Clyde Barrow in *Bonnie and Clyde*?
A *Faye Dunaway and Warren Beatty*

No. 62 Hidden Titles–7

Within each of these dialogues are hidden eight play or playlet titles. How many can you spot–and which famous dramatist wrote each group?

Team A

(He is tense, preoccupied. Perhaps his life is in danger. She is tearful, worried. They have been lovers for some months–but now it seems to be ending...)

She Relax. You're walking up and down like a cat on a hot tin roof.

He (*Angry*) Holy summer and smoke! You–(*More gently*) You don't understand, Rose, my sweet bird of youth.

She I do, I do. I've always understood. Ever since, suddenly, last summer, one night I realized what you meant to me–

He That night! The night we watched that little lizard–

She (*Laughing*) The night of the iguana, you called it.

He (*Angry*) It's all changed now.

She What's got into you? This is the strangest romance.

He I want to keep you away from it all.

She So this is the start of the long goodbye?

He Yes, Rose. Ta-too for now. Ta-too for ever.

Team B

(They are an elderly couple with a shared past; perhaps Cockney, perhaps Northern)

She This is just like old times. Sitting here in the basement. You and me. I mean, listen.

He What to?

She Silence. Pure silence. You know, I feel...contentment.

He I don't know about you. I've got a slight ache.

She You're always grumbling. (*Pause*) What's the matter anyway?

He You know. (*Embarrassed*) Trouble in the works.

She Oh that. What brought it on again?

He Having a night out, I shouldn't wonder. It was a bit of a do, one way and another. There was the dumb waiter–

She What? At the birthday party? You want to take care, you do.

No. 62 Answers

Team A titles
Cat on a Hot Tin Roof
Summer and Smoke
Sweet Bird of Youth
Suddenly Last Summer
The Night of the Iguana
The Strangest Romance (an early one-acter)
The Long Goodbye
The Rose Tattoo
and their author is Tennessee Williams

Team B titles
Old Times
The Basement
Silence
A Slight Ache
Trouble in the Works
A Night Out
The Dumb Waiter
The Birthday Party
and their author is Harold Pinter

No. 63 Carry On Laughing

Another round of questions about television's situation comedies.

In the long-running *Dad's Army* series...

a1 ...which character often claimed 'We're doomed, all doomed'?

b1 *...which character shouted 'Don't panic'?*

a2 ...who played Godfrey?

b2 *...who played the ARP Warden?*

a3 In *George and Mildred*, who played George?

b3 *And who played Mildred?*

a4 What was George and Mildred's surname?

b4 *And in which London suburb were they supposed to live?*

a5 In *The Good Life*, who played Margot?

b5 *And who played Jerry?*

a6 What was the surname of the characters played by Richard Briers and Felicity Kendal?

b6 *And what was their neighbour's surname?*

a7 In *Porridge*, what was the name of the chief warder (with the sergeant-major manner)?

b7 *And what were Fletcher's first names?*

a8 Who got star billing in *On the Buses*?

b8 *Who starred in* Bless This House*?*

a9 In *It Ain't Half Hot Mum*, who played the sergeant-major?

b9 *In* Whatever Happened to the Likely Lads?*, to whom was Terry engaged?*

a10 Who was the star of *Up Pompeii!*?

b10 *What was the name of the character he played?*

a11 Who played teacher Bernard Hedges in *Please Sir!*?

b11 *Which class did he teach?*

a12 Who played the school caretaker?

b12 *Which subsequent series featured some of* Please Sir*'s main characters?*

No. 63 Answers

a1 Frazer
b1 *Corporal Jones*
a2 Arnold Ridley
b2 *Bill Pertwee*
a3 Brian Murphy
b3 *Yootha Joyce*
a4 Roper
b4 *Hampton Wick*
a5 Penelope Keith
b5 *Paul Eddington*
a6 Good
b6 *Leadbetter*
a7 Mr MacKay
b7 *Norman Stanley*
a8 Reg Varney
b8 *Sidney James (with Diana Coupland)*
a9 Windsor Davies
b9 *Thelma*
a10 Frankie Howerd
b10 *Lurcio (the slave)*
a11 John Alderton
b11 *5c*
a12 Deryck Guyler
b12 The Fenn Street Gang

Tie-breaker

Q 'Gerald Wiley' wrote scripts for the show *The Two Ronnies*.
   Whose pen name was 'Gerald Wiley'?
A *Ronnie Barker*

No. 64 Box Office

Where in the British Isles would you be if you were buying tickets at these theatres (or group of theatres)?

a1   The Aldelphi, the Albery and the Aldwych?

b1   *The Swan, the Other Place and the Royal Shakespeare?*

a2   The Grand, the Opera House and the North Pier?

b2   *The Royal, the Dome and the Gardner Centre?*

a3   The Crucible?

b3   *The Citizens (known as the 'Citz')?*

a4   The West Yorkshire Playhouse?

b4   *The Empire, the Playhouse and the Everyman?*

a5   The Abbey, the Gate and the Gaiety?

b5   *The Kings, the Lyceum and the Traverse?*

a6   The Arts and the ADC?

b6   *The Maddermarket and the Theatre Royal?*

a7   The Gulbenkian and the Marlowe?

b7   *The Library and the Royal Exchange?*

a8   The Yvonne Arnaud?

b8   *The Stephen Joseph?*

a9   The Belgrade?

b9   *Spring Street Theatre?*

a10   The Northcott?

b10   *The Wolsey?*

In London, which theatre...

a11   ...situated in Rosebery Avenue has been known for staging opera and ballet?

b11   *...contains an auditorium called 'The Pit'?*

a12   ...was opened in 1891 as a home for the Gilbert and Sullivan operas?

b12   *...is situated in Hammersmith?*

No. 64 Answers

a1 London
b1 *Stratford-upon-Avon*
a2 Blackpool
b2 *Brighton*
a3 Sheffield
b3 *Glasgow*
a4 Leeds
b4 *Liverpool*
a5 Dublin
b5 *Edinburgh*
a6 Cambridge
b6 *Norwich*
a7 Canterbury
b7 *Manchester*
a8 Guildford
b8 *Scarborough*
a9 Coventry
b9 *Hull (Kingston-upon-Hull)*
a10 Exeter
b10 *Ipswich*
a11 Sadler's Wells
b11 *The Barbican*
a12 The Savoy
b12 *The Lyric, Hammersmith (accept: Riverside)*

Tie-breaker

Q Which London theatre was famously managed by Lilian Bayliss?
A *The Old Vic*

No. 65 Get the Guest–4

How many clues do you need before you can identify each of the following stars of the big screen? (See page 9.)

Guest A

1 I never really thought of myself as a sex symbol–more as a comedienne who could dance.
2 I worked my way to stardom in the Forties through a long string of 'B' movies.
3 Famously, I once did a striptease–and removed just one black glove.

Guest B

1 Doris Day said I was a completely private person and there was no way in.
2 I was a matinée idol who had five wives.
3 In my films, I've brought up baby, gone north by northwest and walked, not run.

Guest C

1 Someone once called me a cross between Donald Duck and a Stradivarius.
2 I once said 'Acting is the most minor of gifts. After all, Shirley Temple could do it when she was four.'
3 I've been *Woman of the Year* and up the Congo with Humphrey Bogart.

Guest D

1 I said of myself I'm no actor and never have been.
2 My ears, it was said, made me look like a taxicab with the doors wide open.
3 It happened one night: I beheld the walls of Jerusalem.

No. 65 Answers

Guest A Rita Hayworth (1918–1987)
She was a distant cousin of Ginger Rogers and followed in her father's footsteps as a dancer. She signed a contract with Twentieth Century-Fox and appeared in various B-pictures. Later she was given better roles, and starred with Fred Astaire. In the film *Gilda* (1946) she played the title role. It was in this film she sensuously removed one glove.

Guest B Cary Grant(1904–1986)
He was leading man to such stars as Marlene Dietrich and Mae West. He excelled in comedies such as *Bringing Up Baby* (1938). Alfred Hitchcock cast him in *Suspicion* (1941) and the two men collaborated on *To Catch a Thief* (1955) and *North By Northwest* (1959). His last acting appearance was in *Walk Don't Run* (1966).

Guest C Katharine Hepburn (1907–)
She made her stage début in 1928 and continued to pursue a career in the theatre until an appearance in *The Warrior's Husband* led to her screen début in 1932. *Woman of the Year* was a 1942 film and she appeared in *The African Queen* (1951) with Humphrey Bogart.

Guest D Clark Gable (1901–1960)
After early work on Broadway, his appearance in *The Last Mile* (1930) won him a screen-test. His dignified final performance in *The Misfits* (1961) is perhaps his greatest screen achievement. It was Howard Hughes who said Clark Gable's ears made him look like a taxicab with the doors open. His co-star in *It Happened One Night* (1934) was Claudette Colbert. When they share a tent one night, Gable's character puts up a blanket as a wall between them and utters the famous line, 'Behold the walls of Jericho!'

No. 66 Odd One Out–2

Team A
Here are three speeches which sound as if they might have been written by Norwegian dramatist, Henrik Ibsen–but only two are genuine. Which is the impostor and do you know where the true ones come from?

Ibsen Speech 1
It's the truth, Torvald. When I lived with papa, he used to tell me what he thought about everything, so that I never had any opinions but his. And if I did have any of my own, I kept them quiet, because he wouldn't have liked them. He called me his little doll, and he played with me just the way I played with my dolls. Then I came here to live in your house.

Ibsen Speech 2
Had it not been for that fire, I may not have had the opportunity to build homes for people–for human beings. Comfortable, decent homes, full of light, where parents and children could live in security, and with a genuine feeling of happiness for being born into this world. And–most important of all–with a feeling of neighbourliness, of belonging–belonging to each other–not only in a larger sense, but in little things as well.

Ibsen Speech 3
I tell you Mrs Alving, papa is in an agony of regret and remorse. He was out in the boat, you see, and he shot her–but with his affliction, papa doesn't see very well, you know that?–she was only wounded. Shot in the wing, so she couldn't fly. But the dog, such a wonderful dog is papa's, the dog dived in after the duck and fetched it out of the water. And I am going to pray that the duck may recover, for it is the most precious creature to me in the world.

(Answer on page 253)

Team B

Here are three speeches which might or might not have been written by Oscar Wilde. Which is the impostor—and from which plays do the other two come?

Wilde Speech 1

My dear nieces—you know the Savile girls, don't you—such nice domestic creatures—plain, dreadfully plain,—but so good—well, they're always at the window doing fancy work, and making ugly things for the poor, which I think so useful of them in these dreadful socialist days, and this terrible woman has taken a house in Curzon Street, right opposite them—such a respectable street, too! I don't know what we're coming to. And they tell me *he* goes there four and five times a week. And although they never talk scandal, they—well of course—they remark on it to everyone.

Wilde Speech 2

She, poor child, like all women, will be as careless in her choice of a second husband as she was in her first. She simply cannot appreciate there is no sin but stupidity and so she has become bewitched by Grigsby: that is her lot. His is to be a mere prose Tennyson—as of course was Tennyson. Grigsby does, I grant you, know the precise moment when to say nothing but, rest assured, he will say it at length. Indeed, I have often heard him speak of his own superiority to writers greater than himself—and that is the only imaginative thought he is known to have expressed.

Wilde Speech 3

The English can't stand a man who is always saying he is in the right, but they are very fond of man who admits that he has been in the wrong. It is one of the best things in them. However, in your case, a confession would not do. The money, if you will allow me to say so, is...awkward. Besides, if you did make a clean breast of the whole affair, you would never be able to talk morality again. And in England a man who can't talk morality twice a week to a large, popular, immoral audience is quite over as serious politician.

(Answer on page 254)

No. 67 Modern Musicals

All these musicals have been West End hits in the last 20 years. Can you identify them from these clues?

a1 Performers audition for roles in a musical
b1 *A barber's chair in a murderous 'food factory'*
a2 Set in Saigon, it up-dates the Madame Butterfly story
b2 *A musical with a railway theme and a cast on roller-skates*
a3 Cameron Mackintosh and the Royal Shakespeare Company co-produced this spectacular based on a Victor Hugo story
b3 *Harry Secombe has been associated with this musical version of a Charles Dickens novel*
a4 Twin brothers grow up in very different social backgrounds
b4 *A Clarke Peters musical about five men*
a5 'Hey Look Me Over' was just one hit in this Cy Coleman circus musical
b5 *Julia McKenzie starred in the West End production of this Sondheim panto-style musical*
a6 Hannibal and slave girls, theatrical tricks and (originally) Michael Crawford have all been part of this Lloyd Webber show
b6 *Another Lloyd Webber show, which features couples in love in a variety of situations*
a7 A biographical tribute to a 1950s Texan rock 'n' roll star
b7 *A biographical tribute to a singer known as 'the King'*
a8 Cy Coleman's send-up of 1940s private eye movies
b8 *Tommy Steele starred in this musical version of a Billy Wilder film which had starred Marilyn Monroe*
a9 A John Kander/Fred Ebb musical about a gay prisoner who acts out old movies
b9 *An Andrew Lloyd Webber show based on a Gloria Swanson movie*
a10 A Tim Rice show about a twelfth-century wandering minstrel
b10 *Feathers, assegais and lots of African rhythms were all in this long-running show*

No. 67 Answers

a1   *A Chorus Line*
b1   Sweeney Todd–the Demon Barber of Fleet Street
a2   *Miss Saigon*
b2   Starlight Express
a3   *Les Miserables*
b3   Pickwick
a4   *Blood Brothers*
b4   Five Guys Named Moe
a5   *Barnum*
b5   Into the Woods
a6   *Phantom of the Opera*
b6   Aspects of Love
a7   *Buddy* (Buddy Holly)
b7   Elvis
a8   *City of Angels*
b8   Some Like It Hot
a9   *Kiss of the Spider Woman*
b9   Sunset Boulevard
a10 *Blondel*
b10 Ipi Tombi

Tie-breaker

Q   When the film musical *Singin' in the Rain* had its London stage première in 1983, who directed it and played the Gene Kelly role?

A   *Tommy Steele*

No. 68 Television Crime

A round about television crime series.

a1   Which detective has been played by Rupert Davies and Michael Gambon?

b1   *Who wrote the novels on which the series were based?*

a2   In which city was Inspector Morse based?

b2   *Who wrote the novels on which the series was based?*

a3   What was his 'sidekick' called?

b3   *Who played him?*

a4   Who took on the role of Poirot in 1989?

b4   *Who wrote the novels on which the series was based?*

a5   Who played Chief Inspector Wexford?

b5   *And who wrote the novels that inspired the series?*

a6   What is the name of Poirot's 'sidekick'?

b6   *And what is the name of Wexford's assistant?*

a7   In which crime series did Michael Brandon play a New York cop on attachment to Britain?

b7   *Which American crime series featured Crockett and Tubbs?*

a8   *And who played Crockett?*

b8   In *Dempsey and Makepeace*, who played Makepeace

a9   In which county was the *Heartbeat* series set?

b9   *In which decade was it set?*

a10   Who played the village constable, Nick Rowan?

b10   *In which soap opera had he previously appeared?*

a11   In which television series did Detective Chief Superintendent Lockhart work for Scotland Yard?

b11   *Who played him?*

a12   In which city was the drama *GBH* set?

b12   *Who wrote it?*

No. 68 Answers

a1 Maigret
b1 *(Georges) Simenon*
a2 Oxford
b2 *Colin Dexter*
a3 Sgt Lewis
b3 *Kevin Whatley*
a4 David Suchet
b4 *Agatha Christie*
a5 George Baker
b5 *Ruth Rendell*
a6 Captain Hastings
b6 *Inspector Mike Burden*
a7 *Dempsey and Makepeace*
b7 Miami Vice
a8 *Don Johnson*
b8 Glynis Barber
a9 Yorkshire
b9 *The Sixties*
a10 Nick Berry
b10 EastEnders
a11 *No Hiding Place*
b11 *Raymond Francis*
a12 Liverpool
b12 *Alan Bleasdale*

Tie-breaker

Q In which series was Laura Palmer killed?
A Twin Peaks

No. 69 Big Screen Crime

Which criminal or criminals were portrayed in...

a1 ...*The Scarface Mob*?

b1 ...A Study in Terror?

a2 ...*10 Rillington Place*?

b2 ...Birdman of Alcatraz?

Who was the comic policeman or detective in...

a3 ...*The Pink Panther*?

b3 ...Easy Street?

a4 ...*On the Beat*?

b4 ...Ask a Policeman?

Who played...

a5 ...Hercule Poirot in *Death on the Nile*?

b5 ...Hercule Poirot in Murder on the Orient Express?

a6 ...Miss Marple in *Murder She Said* and *Murder at the Gallop*?

b6 ...Philip Marlowe in the 1946 version of The Big Sleep?

a7 ...Sherlock Holmes in *The Adventures of Sherlock Holmes* (1939)?

b7 ...Sherlock Holmes in The Private Life of Sherlock Holmes (1969)?

a8 In which film did Mel Gibson play a highly disturbed policeman?

b8 In which film did Police Officer Murphy's innards become encased in metal?

a9 In which city was the jewel robbery attempted in *Topkapi*?

b9 And where did thieves attempt a robbery in The Italian Job?

a10 Which Hollywood 'tough guy' played a San Francisco detective in the film *Bullitt*?

b10 And who played a leather-jacketed 'psycho' in Stanley Kramer's The Wild One?

a11 Which oriental detective has been played by Warner Oland in 16 films and by Sidney Toler in 22 films?

b11 What sport was played by the gentleman thief Raffles?

a12 In which film about 'rookie' cops did Steve Guttenberg (say: Gootenberg) star in 1984?

b12 In which 1985 film did Harrison Ford play a cop involved in a murder and a Christian sect?

No. 69 Answers

a1 Al Capone's gang
b1 *Jack the Ripper*
a2 (John) Christie (hanged in 1953 for the murder of his wife and five other women)
b2 *Robert Stroud (a murderer who studied birds while in prison)*
a3 Peter Sellers
b3 *Charlie Chaplin*
a4 Norman Wisdom
b4 *Will Hay*
a5 Peter Ustinov
b5 *Albert Finney*
a6 Margaret Rutherford
b6 *Humphrey Bogart*
a7 Basil Rathbone
b7 *Robert Stephens*
a8 *Lethal Weapon*
b8 Robocop
a9 Istanbul
b9 *Turin*
a10 Steve McQueen
b10 *Marlon Brando*
a11 Charlie Chan
b11 *Cricket*
a12 *Police Academy*
b12 Witness

Tie-breaker

Q Which 1948 film, set in Manhattan, starred Barry Fitzgerald as Lieutenant Muldoon leading a homicide squad–and concluded with the words, 'There are eight million stories in...'?

A The Naked City *(the concluding words were '...in the naked city. This has been one of them.')*

No. 70 Where's That From?–3

All these lines come from classics of the cinema–but who said them, and in which film?

a1   'Here's lookin' at you, kid.'
b1   *'We need a bigger boat.'*
a2   'I vant to be alone.'
b2   *'Martha, will you show her where we keep the...er, euphemism?'*
a3   'Your mother can't be with you anymore.'
b3   *'Mrs Robinson, you're trying to seduce me, aren't you?'*
a4   'Mother–what's the phrase?–isn't quite herself today.'
b4   *'Greed is good! Greed is right! Greed works!'*
a5   'We rob banks.'
b5   *'That's quite a dress you almost have on.'*
a6   'Who *are* those guys?'
b6   *'Is that a gun in your pocket or are you just glad to see me?'*
a7   'Give me a girl at an impressionable age and she is mine for life.'
b7   *'God Bless Captain Vere!'*
a8   'Where the devil are my slippers, Liza?'
b8   *'Beulah, peel me a grape.'*
a9   'I'll have what she's having.'
b9   *'If I'd have forgotten myself with that girl, I'd remember it.'*
a10 'Ya wanna dance or would you rather just suck face?'
b10 *'Frankly, my dear, I don't give a damn!'*

No. 70 Answers

a1 Humphrey Bogart to Ingrid Bergman in *Casablanca* (1942)

b1 *Roy Scheider to Robert Shaw on first sighting the shark in* Jaws *(1975)*

a2 Greta Garbo to John Barrymore in *Grand Hotel* (1932)

b2 *Richard Burton to Elizabeth Taylor regarding Sandy Dennis' trip to the...er, bathroom in* Who's Afraid of Virginia Woolf? *(1966)*

a3 The Great Prince bringing bad news to Bambi in *Bambi* (1942)

b3 *Dustin Hoffman to Anne Bancroft in* The Graduate *(1967)*

a4 Anthony Perkins to Janet Leigh in *Psycho* (1960)

b4 *Michael Douglas in* Wall Street *(1987)*

a5 Warren Beatty and Faye Dunaway's description of their job in *Bonnie and Clyde* (1967)

b5 *Gene Kelly to Nina Foch in* An American in Paris *(1951)*

a6 Robert Redford's frequent query to Paul Newman regarding the posse on their trail in *Butch Cassidy and the Sundance Kid* (1969)

b6 *Mae West to Charles Osgood in* She Done Him Wrong *(1933)*

a7 Maggie Smith's credo in *The Prime of Miss Jean Brodie* (1969)

b7 *Terence Stamp to Peter Ustinov in* Billy Budd *(1962)*

a8 Rex Harrison to Audrey Hepburn in *My Fair Lady* (1964)

b8 *Mae West to Gertrude Howard in* I'm No Angel *(1933)*

a9 Estelle Reiner after watching Meg Ryan in *When Harry Met Sally* (1989)

b9 *Fred Astaire in* Top Hat *(1935)*

a10 Henry Fonda to Katharine Hepburn in *On Golden Pond* (1981)

b10 *Clark Gable to Vivien Leigh in* Gone with the Wind *(1939)*

Tie-breaker

Q In which 1942 film does a camel say to camera, 'This is the screwiest picture I was ever in'?

A Road to Morocco

No. 71 Stars of the Seventies

Can you complete this cast list to show who played each of these roles in famous films of the Seventies?

a1   Don Corleone, the Mafia boss, in *The Godfather*?
b1   *'Dirty Harry' in* Dirty Harry?
a2   McCabe in *McCabe and Mrs Miller*?
b2   *Mrs Miller in* McCabe and Mrs Miller?
a3   The father in *Kramer vs Kramer*?
b3   *And who played his ex-wife?*
a4   Rocky in *Rocky*?
b4   *The singer moving up the career ladder in* A Star Is Born?
a5   Yossarian in *Catch-22*?
b5   *Major Major in* Catch-22?
a6   Detective 'Popeye' Doyle in *The French Connection*?
b6   *Russo in the same film?*
a7   A former Nazi, working in New York as a dentist, in *Marathon Man*?
b7   *The head of the Institute for the Very, Very Nervous in* High Anxiety?
a8   Gatsby in *The Great Gatsby*?
b8   *Daisy in* The Great Gatsby?
a9   Philip Marlowe in the 1973 up-date of *The Long Goodbye*?
b9   *The upper-class English 'hit-man' in* The Day of the Jackal?
a10   Mad Max in *Mad Max*?
b10   *Klute in* Klute?
a11   The village schoolmaster's wife in *Ryan's Daughter*?
b11   *Alex in* The Clockwork Orange?
a12   Private investigator J. J. Gittes in *Chinatown*?
b12   *The taxi driver in* Taxi Driver?

No. 71 Answers

a1   Marlon Brando
b1   *Clint Eastwood*
a2   Warren Beatty
b2   *Julie Christie*
a3   Dustin Hoffman
b3   *Meryl Streep*
a4   Sylvester Stallone
b4   *Barbra Streisand*
a5   Alan Arkin
b5   *Bob Newhart*
a6   Gene Hackman
b6   *Roy Scheider*
a7   Laurence Olivier
b7   *Mel Brooks*
a8   Robert Redford
b8   *Mia Farrow*
a9   Elliott Gould
b9   *Edward Fox*
a10   Mel Gibson
b10   *Donald Sutherland*
a11   Sarah Miles
b11   *Malcolm McDowell*
a12   Jack Nicholson
b12   *Robert de Niro*

Tie-breaker

Q   Who played the two young lovers in *Love Story*?
A   *Ali MacGraw and Ryan O'Neal*

No. 72 Hidden Titles–8

Within each of these dialogues are hidden the titles of nine songs from musicals. Can you spot the titles and say who wrote each group of shows?

Team A

(*She is a Joyce Grenfell-like infant teacher; he's a precocious little brat.*)

Teacher Now, as I told you, I'm taking you on a nature ramble. In the woods. In the evening.

Brat Please miss, you don't have to.

Teacher (*Excessively cheerful*) My dearest dear, it's no trouble. My life belongs to you.

Brat (*Aside*) Such vitality! (*Aloud*) What if it rains?

Teacher It's bound to be right on the night.

Brat On such a night as this one, we'd get very wet.

Teacher I shall magic the weather. Yes I shall. (*Conspiratorial*) I can give you the starlight.

Brat Please, miss. Someone's taken my coat.

Teacher (*Breezily*) Finder, please return. (*Storytelling*) Now it's going to be a really glamorous night–

Brat What will there be to do in the woods?

Teacher Lots of things. We'll gather flowers. We'll gather... lilacs!

Team B

Precise Young Lady Excuse me, with a little bit of luck, you must be the bus inspector?

Drunk Hullo, lady. No, I'm an ordinary man.

Lady You see, I want to catch a bus to St Paul's.

Drunk Ah, there but for you go I!

Lady What do you mean by that?

Drunk You my darling, you are the love of my life.

Lady Really, you haven't a clue how to handle a woman!

Drunk Handle a...!!! Now wouldn't it be loverly–

Lady Just you wait!

Drunk From this day on, I'll wait for ever.

Lady All I'm waiting for is a bus that'll get me to the church on time.

No. 72 Answers

Team A titles
'My Dearest Dear' from *The Dancing Years*
'Vitality' from *Gay's the Word*
'My Life Belongs To You' from *The Dancing Years*
'It's Bound To Be Right On the Night' from *Gay's the Word*
'On Such a Night As This' from *Gay's the Word*
'I Can Give You the Starlight' from *The Dancing Years*
'Finder, Please Return' from *Gay's the Word*
'Glamorous Night' from *Glamorous Night*
'We'll Gather Lilacs' from *Perchance to Dream*
And they were all written by Ivor Novello

Team B titles
'With a Little Bit of Luck' from *My Fair Lady*
'I'm an Ordinary Man' from *My Fair Lady*
'There But For You Go I' from *Brigadoon*
'The Love of My Life' from *Brigadoon*
'How To Handle a Woman' from *Camelot*
'Wouldn't It Be Loverly' from *My Fair Lady*
'Just You Wait' from *My Fair Lady*
'From This Day On' from *Brigadoon*
'Get Me To the Church On Time' from *My Fair Lady*
And they were all written by Alan J. Lerner (words) and Frederick Loewe (music)

Tie-breaker

Q For what is 'Corgi and Bess' a nickname?
A *The Queen's Christmas broadcast*

No. 73 TV's Famous Faces

a1 Who introduced *The Six Five Special*?
b1 *Who was the most famous presenter of* The Old Grey Whistle Test?
a2 Who played the organ and introduced *Stars on Sunday*?
b2 *Who offered the invitation 'Swingalong with me'*?
a3 Who was the original presenter of *New Faces*?
b3 *Who presented it when it was revived in 1989*?
a4 Who introduced *The Sky's the Limit*?
b4 *And who made a comeback with* The Wheel of Fortune?

With which television star do you associate...
a5 ...a rocking chair and comfy pullover?
b5 *...Hill's Angels*?
a6 ...crime-busting from a wheelchair?
b6 *...the 'clap-ometer'*?

On what subject were the following experts...
a7 ...Arthur Negus?
b7 *...Barry Bucknell*?
a8 ...Philip Harben?
b8 *...George Cansdale*?

What programme or job have (or had) these in common...
a9 ...Robert Dougall, Richard Baker and Kenneth Kendall?
b9 *...Robert Robinson, Barry Took and Anne Robinson*?
a10 ...Emlyn Hughes, Bill Beaumont and Ian Botham?
b10 *...The Bachelors, Les Dawson and Little and Large*?
a11 ...Margot Bryant, Lynne Carol and Violet Carson?
b11 *...Peter Ustinov, Albert Finney and David Suchet*?
a12 ...Sylvia Peters, Mary Malcolm and McDonald Hobley?
b12 *...Geoffrey Johnson Smith, Derek Hart and Alan Whicker*?

No. 73 Answers

a1 Pete Murray (and Josephine Douglas)
b1 *('Whispering') Bob Harris*
a2 Jess Yates
b2 *Max Bygraves*
a3 Derek Hobson
b3 *Marti Caine*
a4 Hughie Green
b4 *Michael Miles*
a5 Val Doonican
b5 *Benny Hill*
a6 Raymond Burr (as 'Ironside')
b6 *Hughie Green (in* Opportunity Knocks*)*
a7 Antiques
b7 *Do-it-yourself jobs*
a8 Cookery
b8 *Pets (accept: animals)*
a9 All were once BBC newsreaders
b9 *All have presented* Points of View
a10 All have captained teams on *A Question of Sport*
b10 *All were 'discovered' on Hughie Green's* Opportunity Knocks
a11 They played the three old ladies in the 'Snug' in *Coronation Street's* 'Rover's Return' (Minnie Caldwell, Martha Longhurst and Ena Sharples) (accept: *Coronation Street*)
b11 *All have played Agatha Christie's Poirot*
a12 All were BBC announcers (in the Fifties)
b12 *All were regular interviewers on* Tonight

Tie-breaker

Q Can you name the four regular panelists on *What's My Line?* in the mid-Fifties?

A *Lady Isobel Barnett, Barbara Kelly, David Nixon and Gilbert Harding*

No. 74 Follow that Plot–1

Two of Shakespeare's best known plays are *A Midsummer Night's Dream* and *Macbeth*–but can you fill in the gaps in these summaries of what happens in part of each play?

Team A

A Midsummer Night's Dream, Act II, scene i

Puck is an attendant to Oberon, King of the Fairies (who has quarrelled with his queen, ...1...). Oberon and ...1... have come to Athens to bless the wedding of Duke ...2... and Hippolyta, but they are distracted by their quarrel because ...1... will not give up ...3... whom Oberon wants as his page. When ...1... and her servants have departed, Oberon sends his attendant ...4... to fetch a flower whose juice has a magic power. If the juice is squeezed into the eyes of someone who is asleep, that person will fall in love with the first creature he sees on waking. Oberon plans to squeeze the juice in the eyes of ...1..., by way of gaining revenge on her. However, a young Athenian called ...5... enters in pursuit of his love Hermia who has eloped with ...6.... In his turn ...5... is pursued by ...7... even though he is not interested in her. Oberon tells Puck to apply the love-juice to the eyes of ...5... so that he will fall in love again with ...7....

Team B

Macbeth, Act II, scenes ii and iii

Lady Macbeth waits while ...1... murders King Duncan. When she notices he has brought the ...2... with him from the king's room, he refuses to return them. Lady Macbeth does this while ...1... is frightened by a knocking at the front gate. The drunken ...3... imagines he is guarding the gateway to ...4.... When he eventually opens the gate, it is to let in ...5... and Lennox. ...5... goes to wake the king and returns with news of the murder. ...1... and Lennox go to investigate; Lady Macbeth and Banquo enter; and then ...1... returns. Malcolm and ...6... are told of their father's murder and Macbeth announces that in fury he has killed the ...7..., the apparent murderers. Malcolm and ...6... fear they may be the next victims.

No. 74 Answers

Team A
1 Titania
2 Theseus
3 an Indian boy (or 'changeling')
4 Puck (or Robin Goodfellow)
5 Demetrius
6 Lysander
7 Helena

Team B
1 Macbeth
2 daggers
3 porter
4 hell
5 Macduff
6 Donalbain
7 grooms

Tie-breaker

Q In which three Shakespeare plays does Falstaff appear, and in which other play is his death reported?

A Henry IV Part I, Henry IV Part 2 *and* The Merry Wives of Windsor; *his death is described in* Henry V

No. 75 An Actor's Life for Me!

Can you deduce who these theatrical giants are (some of yesteryear, some still marvellously with us)?

a1 A Welsh-born actor who, in the 1950s, seemed likely to reach the pinnacle of his profession but films kept him out of the theatre. He acted on screen with his famous wife

b1 *An English actress and beauty, for many years the wife of Laurence Olivier. On film, she played Scarlett O'Hara*

a2 An English actor who created the roles of Richard III, Hamlet, Othello and Lear. His father built the first English playhouses

b2 *An actress famed for her charm rather than her (theatrical) talent. She retired in 1669 having earlier sold oranges*

a3 An English actress and a star of plays, revue and musicals in Britain and America. She was the original Amanda in *Private Lives*, playing opposite Noël Coward

b3 *An English actress whose definitive performances have been her Lady Bracknell and her Nurse in* Romeo and Juliet

a4 A Black American actor and singer who made his name as Jim Harris in *All God's Chillun Have Wings* (1924) and Joe in *Show Boat* (1928). His was one of the great voices of the century

b4 *A trumpet-toned American actress and singer who starred as Annie in* Annie Get Your Gun. *Her later triumphs included* Call Me Madam *and* Hello, Dolly

a5 An English actor-manager and perhaps the greatest Lear of modern times, his touring company brought Shakespeare to many audiences in Britain and overseas

b5 *An English actor-manager whose Shakespearian productions were both elaborate and realistic, culminating in live rabbits on stage in his* A Midsummer Night's Dream

a6 A Scottish-born actor and revue artist, he was Britain's leading song-and-dance man between the Wars

b6 *An English actress and dancer, she was a major star of musicals between the Wars and was the voice of Mrs Dale on radio!*

No. 75 Answers

a1 Richard Burton (married to Elizabeth Taylor)
b1 *Vivien Leigh*
a2 Richard Burbage
b2 *Nell Gwynn*
a3 Gertrude Lawrence
b3 *Dame Edith Evans*
a4 Paul Robeson
b4 *Ethel Merman*
a5 Sir Donald Wolfit
b5 *Sir Herbert Beerbohm Tree*
a6 Jack Buchanan
b6 *Jessie Matthews*

Tie-breaker

Q Who said, 'I love acting. It's so much more real than life'?
A *Oscar Wilde*

No. 76 Sig Tunes

Which television programme had as its signature tune...
a1 ...'Who Do You Think You Are Kidding, Mr Hitler?'?
b1 ...'An Ordinary Copper'?
a2 ...'The Liberty Bell' (by Sousa)?
b2 ...a theme from 'Spartacus' by Khachaturian?
a3 ...'Hit and Miss'?
b3 ...'Galloping Home'?
a4 ...'Johnny Todd'?
b4 ...'Barnacle Bill'?

In which children's shows would you regularly hear the words...
a5 ...'Feared by the bad, loved by the good...'?
b5 ...'Time to go home, time to go home...'?
a6 ...'Making good use of the things that we find,
       Things that the everyday folks leave behind...'?
b6 ...'Close friends get to call him TC'?

Which radio programme has (or had) as its signature tune...
a7 ...'Barwick Green'?
b7 ...'The Devil's Gallop'?
a8 ...'By the Sleepy Lagoon'?
b8 ...'Parade of the Tin Soldiers'?
a9 ...'With a Song in My Heart'?
b9 ...'Puffin' Billy'?

Whose signature tune was...
a10 ...'Say It with Music'?
b10 ...'In the Mood'?
a11 ...'You're Dancing on My Heart'?
b11 ...'Somebody Stole My Gal'?
a12 ...'Thanks for the Memory'?
b12 ...'I Do Like to be Beside the Seaside'?

No. 76 Answers

a1   *Dad's Army*
b1   Dixon of Dock Green
a2   *Monty Python's Flying Circus*
b2   The Onedin Line
a3   *Juke Box Jury*
b3   Black Beauty
a4   *Z-Cars*
b4   Blue Peter
a5   *The Adventures of Robin Hood*
b5   Andy Pandy *(in* Watch with Mother*)*
a6   *The Wombles* ('Wombling Free')
b6   Boss Cat *(known as* Top Cat *in America)*
a7   *The Archers*
b7   Dick Barton–Special Agent
a8   *Desert Island Discs*
b8   Toytown
a9   *Two Way Family Favourites*
b9   Children's Choice
a10 Jack Payne
b10 *Joe Loss*
a11 Victor Sylvester
b11 *Billy Cotton*
a12 Bob Hope
b12 *Reginald Dixon (Blackpool Tower Ballroom's organist)*

Tie-breaker

Q   Which duo (who had a 1993 revival) sang:
'It's you for me and me for you,
Just as one and one make two,
It's us until forever...'?
A   *Pinky and Perky*

164

No. 77 Music, Book and Lyrics

Who wrote the music for these shows...
a1   ...*West Side Story?*
b1   ...Show Boat?
a2   ...*Porgy and Bess?*
b2   ...The King and I?
a3   ...*Can Can* and *High Society?*
b3   ...Paint Your Wagon *and* Gigi?
a4   ...*Oliver!?*
b4   ...Salad Days?
a5   ...*Call Me Madam?*
b5   ...Me and My Girl?
a6   ...*Cabaret?*
b6   ...A Chorus Line?
a7   ...*Miss Saigon?*
b7   ...Hello, Dolly?

Who wrote the lyrics for...
a8   ...*The Sound of Music?*
b8   ...My Fair Lady?
a9   ...*Cats?*
b9   ...Jesus Christ Superstar?
a10   ...*Starlight Express?*
b10   ...Blood Brothers?

Who wrote the music, book and lyrics for...
a11   ...*The Boy Friend?*
b11   ...Perchance to Dream?
a12   ...*Bitter Sweet?*
b12   ...The Most Happy Fella?

No. 77 Answers

a1   Leonard Bernstein
b1   *Jerome Kern*
a2   George Gershwin
b2   *Richard Rodgers*
a3   Cole Porter
b3   *Frederick Loewe*
a4   Lionel Bart
b4   *Julian Slade*
a5   Irving Berlin
b5   *Noel Gay*
a6   John Kander
b6   *Marvin Hamlisch*
a7   Alain Boublil and Claude-Michel Schönberg
b7   *Jerry Herman*
a8   Oscar Hammerstein II
b8   *Alan Jay Lerner*
a9   T. S. Eliot (some additional material by Trevor Nunn)
b9   *Tim Rice*
a10 Richard Stilgoe
b10 *Willy Russell*
a11 Sandy Wilson
b11 *Ivor Novello*
a12 Noël Coward
b12 *Frank Loesser*

Tie-breaker

Q Who composed the music for the 1926 show *The Desert Song*?
A *Sigmund Romberg*

No. 78 Babies, Brutes and Dollies

Television production seems to generate its own language which can sometimes be quite incomprehensible to outsiders. How many of these terms can you explain?

a1 Clapperboard?

b1 *Canned laughter?*

a2 Live?

b2 *A clip?*

a3 FX?

b3 *Autocue?*

a4 A 'promo' or promotion?

b4 *A boom?*

a5 Long shot?

b5 *BCU?*

a6 ENG?

b6 *Day for night?*

a7 To pan?

b7 *A dolly?*

a8 The can (as in 'It's in the can')?

b8 *Cans?*

a9 To crab?

b9 *The grid?*

a10 Cherrypicker?

b10 *Apple boxes?*

a11 A brute?

b11 *A baby?*

a12 The cue dot?

b12 *Letterbox?*

No. 78 Answers

a1   The hinged board bearing the details of a film take which is clapped together to provide identification and to synchronize sound and picture at the start of action

b1   *Pre-recorded, added laughter*

a2   Transmission as events actually happen

b2   *A short film sequence*

a3   Effects (usually sound)

b3   *A device which projects a rolling commentary in front of a programme presenter or news reader. He or she can read it without dropping his or her eyes from the lens of the camera*

a4   A trailer for a forthcoming programme

b4   *A telescopic arm from which microphones can hang*

a5   Extreme distance in a camera shot (e.g. of scenery)

b5   *Big Close Up–when the actor's features fill the screen*

a6   Electronic News Gathering: a system which, instead of a normal film camera, uses a small portable video camera

b6   *Filming night scenes in daylight using special filters in the camera*

a7   To move the camera in a horizontal arc

b7   *A wheeled mounting for a camera to allow it to move freely*

a8   A round metal box to hold reels of film

b8   *Headphones*

a9   To move the camera sideways

b9   *Lattice metal 'ceiling' in a studio from which lighting and monitors are suspended*

a10   An hydraulically-operated tower for high angle location camera work

b10   *Wooden boxes used to raise the height of properties or small actors*

a11   A large focusing spot lamp, between 15k and 22.5k

b11   *A small spotlight, usually 750w*

a12   A small flickering square electronically inlaid in the top right-hand corner of the television picture before the commercial break. It is usually switched off at the start of the 'End of Part' caption

b12   *An electronically laid oblong, carrying information at the bottom of the screen*

No. 79 Movie Brats and the Brat Pack

In the Seventies, a group of new young directors were nicknamed the 'Movie Brats'. In the Eighties, a group of young actors were labelled the 'Brat Pack'. How much do you know about them and their films?

a1 Who played Indiana Jones in *Indiana Jones and the Last Crusade*?
b1 *And who played his father?*
a2 Who was Susan in *Desperately Seeking Susan*?
b2 *And who played Axel Foley in* Beverly Hills Cop*?*
a3 Who was the star of *The Karate Kid*?
b3 *Whose son Michael starred in* Wall Street*?*
a4 Who was the male star of *Dirty Dancing*?
b4 *And in which 1983 film did he star with Tom Cruise, Ralph Macchio and Emilio Estevez?*

In which film did...
a5 ...Jeff Goldblum get changed into an insect?
b5 *...Tom Cruise play a gung-ho pilot?*
a6 ...Meg Ryan meet Billy Crystal?
b6 *...Robin Williams play an English literature teacher?*
a7 ...Jodie Foster play a rape victim?
b7 *...Robert de Niro play a self-destructive boxer?*
a8 ...a military robot get struck by lightning and come to life?
b8 *...a group of Chicago high school students have to write an essay one Saturday morning?*

Who directed...
a9 ...*The Last Temptation of Christ*?
b9 ...The Godfather*?*
a10 ...*American Graffiti*?
b10 ...Indiana Jones and the Temple of Doom?
a11 ...*Dillinger*?
b11 ...Carrie *and* Phantom of the Paradise*?*
a12 ...*Apocalypse Now*?
b12 *...Mean Streets?*

No. 79 Answers

a1   Harrison Ford
b1   *Sean Connery*
a2   Madonna
b2   *Eddie Murphy*
a3   Ralph Macchio
b3   *Kirk Douglas (actor Michael Douglas being his son)*
a4   Patrick Swayze
b4   The Outsiders
a5   *The Fly*
b5   Top Gun
a6   *When Harry Met Sally...* (they played the leading roles)
b6   Dead Poets Society
a7   *The Accused*
b7   Raging Bull
a8   *Short Circuit*
b8   The Breakfast Club
a9   Martin Scorsese
b9   *Francis (Ford) Coppola*
a10   George Lucas
b10   *Steven Spielberg*
a11   John Milius
b11   *Brian de Palma*
a12   Francis (Ford) Coppola
b12   *Martin Scorsese*

Tie-breaker

Q   In which 'sci-fi' film did Matthew Broderick and Ally Sheedy play teenagers trying to avert World War 3?

A   War Games

No. 80 Messy Deaths

In stage plays, how does each of the following meet his or her death?

a1 Cleopatra?
b1 *Polonius?*
a2 Falstaff?
b2 *Pirelli?*
a3 Bunberry?
b3 *Daisy Renton?*
a4 Cinna the Poet?
b4 *Brand?*
a5 Pyramus?
b5 *Edward II?*
a6 Desdemona?
b6 *Faustus?*
a7 Sister George?
b7 *Demetrius and Chiron?*
a8 Willy Loman?
b8 *Cordelia?*
a9 Laius?
b9 *Laertes?*

Tie-breaker

Q On television's *Coronation Street*, how did Alan Bradley meet his death?
A *He was killed by a Blackpool tram*

No. 80 Answers

a1   She commits suicide by holding an asp (a poisonous snake) to her bosom in Shakespeare's *Antony and Cleopatra*

b1   *He is stabbed behind an arras (a screen) in Shakespeare's* Hamlet

a2   He is said to have died of a broken heart, after Prince Hal has given up his company on becoming king (*Henry V* by Shakespeare)

b2   *He is butchered by Sweeney Todd's razor (and subsequently turned into meat pies) in* Sweeney Todd

a3   He is exploded ('Bunberry is exploded') in *The Importance of Being Earnest* by Oscar Wilde (He is a non-existent character who is no longer needed to provide an alibi)

b3   *She commits suicide in* An Inspector Calls *by J. B. Priestley*

a4   He is lynched by a mob when they mistake him for Cinna the Conspirator in Shakespeare's *Julius Caesar*

b4   *He is killed in an avalanche, caused by a gypsy who believes him to be Christ in* Brand *by Ibsen*

a5   He commits suicide, stabbing himself in the left pap. Pyramus is a character played by Bottom in a play within *A Midsummer Night's Dream* by Shakespeare

b5   *He is assassinated with a red-hot poker in Marlowe's* Edward II

a6   Othello smothers her with a pillow in Shakespeare's *Othello*

b6   *He is torn limb from limb and cast into eternal damnation in* Doctor Faustus *by Marlowe*

a7   She is killed by a van in a road accident (She's a soap opera character within *The Killing of Sister George* by Frank Marcus)

b7   *They are killed by Titus Andronicus and made into a pie in Shakespeare's* Titus Andronicus

a8   He commits suicide in his own car in *Death of a Salesman* by Arthur Miller

b8   *She is hanged in prison in Shakespeare's* King Lear

a9   He is killed by his own son, Œdipus, where three roads meet in Sophocles' *Œdipus Rex*

b9   *He is killed by his own poisoned sword in Shakespeare's* Hamlet

No. 81 What's in a Name?

The following people all chose new names for their screen careers. By what name is each one better known?

a1 Norma Jean Mortenson (or Norma Jean Baker)?

b1 *Virginia Katherine McMath?*

a2 Vivian Mary Hartley?

b2 *Gloria May Josephine Svensson?*

a3 Sofia Villani Scicolone?

b3 *Eddie Israel Itskowitz–who appeared in such films of the Thirties as* Palmy Days *and* Roman Scandals*?*

a4 Joe Yule (who, as a boy, was in the film *Huckleberry Finn*)?

b4 *Arthur Stanley Jefferson (born at Ulverston in the Lake District)?*

a5 Margarita Carmen Cansino

b5 *Dino Crocetti?*

a6 Emanuel Goldenberg?

b6 *Philip Silver?*

a7 Gladys Mary Smith?

b7 *Rodolpho Alfonzo Raffaelo Pierre Filibert Gugliemi di Valentina D'Antonguolla?*

And who has been known by these nicknames?

a8 The Duke?

b8 *The King?*

a9 America's Sweetheart?

b9 *The 'It' Girl?*

a10 The Old Groaner?

b10 *The Platinum Blonde?*

a11 The King of Hollywood?

b11 *The Sex Kitten (a French actress)?*

a12 The Singing Capon?

b12 *Hollywood's Mermaid?*

No. 81 Answers

a1   Marilyn Monroe
b1   *Ginger Rogers*
a2   Vivien Leigh
b2   *Gloria Swanson*
a3   Sophia Loren
b3   *Eddie Cantor*
a4   Mickey Rooney
b4   *Stan Laurel*
a5   Rita Hayworth
b5   *Dean Martin*
a6   Edward G. Robinson
b6   *Phil Silvers*
a7   Mary Pickford
b7   *Rudolph Valentino*
a8   John Wayne
b8   *Elvis Presley*
a9   Mary Pickford
b9   *Clara Bow*
a10   Bing Crosby
b10   *Jean Harlow*
a11   Clark Gable
b11   *Brigitte Bardot*
a12   Nelson Eddy
b12   *Esther Williams*

Tie-breaker

Q   Leonard, Adolph, Julius and Herbert were the real first names of whom?

A   *The Marx Brothers (Chico, Harpo, Groucho and Zeppo respectively)*

No. 82 Hidden Titles–9

Each of these dialogues contains a number of play titles. Can you spot the titles and say who is the author of each group?

Team A

(*Two upper-class, very 'Sloane' young people are desperately in love*)

She Norman. Norman, relatively speaking, it's love after all, isn't it?

He Of course Angela. Of course it is. Time and time again, I've told you. I love you.

She Norman, joking apart, I was wondering–

He Confusions. Confusions, that's what you're trying to introduce into this affair–

She I'm not, I'm not. Dammit all, we're living together. We share all our most...our most intimate exchanges–

He What you want to know is how the other–

She (*Passionate*) What I want to feel is Norman conquests everything!

Team B

(*He is cheerful; she is introspective.*)

He What are you doing, Joanna–sitting in the dark?

She (*Sighs*)

He That's a deep...breath. The fire's almost gone out.

She I was just looking at the embers. Remembering happy days–and waiting.

He Waiting?

She Waiting.

He Waiting for what, eh Jo?

She Waiting for God.

He Waiting for God. Oh. That.

She Don't you believe in hell?

He Not I.

She But all that sin, all that fall must go to–

He That's all make believe. A dead end, if I may say.

She That may sound clever. 'A dead end–'

He –Game set and match to me. Now come and play the piano.

No. 82 Answers

Team A titles
Relatively Speaking
Love After All
Time and Time Again
Joking Apart
Confusions
Living Together
Intimate Exchanges
Norman Conquests
and the playwright is Alan Ayckbourn

Team B titles
Breath
Embers
Happy Days
Eh Joe
Waiting for Godot
Not I
All That Fall
Endgame
Play
and the playwright is Samuel Beckett

No. 83 Commercial Break

A round about ITV—but first, in an advert...

a1 ...why did Gary Myers perform a series of dangerous stunts?

b1 *...which product did a nautical captain first advertise in 1967?*

a2 ...which beer 'refreshes the parts other beers cannot reach'?

b2 *...what did a young man deliver up a cobbled street on his bike?*

a3 ...who were the bowler-hatted men who began picking lumps out of flour in 1965?

b3 *...for whom did Barbara Woodehouse start training sheepdogs in 1964?*

a4 ...who said 'My name is Bond, Brooke Bond'?

b4 *...what did 'Arthur' advertise?*

a5 ...which drink did William Franklyn advertise for 10 years?

b5 *...in which ads did both Mary Holland and Linda Bellingham play Mum?*

a6 ...which drink was associated with the song 'I'd Like to Teach the World to Sing'?

b6 *...and which group recorded the song?*

Welcome back! And now, which commercial television company produced (or produces)...

a7 ...*Tales of the Unexpected*?

b7 *...Brideshead Revisited?*

a8 ...*Crossroads*?

b8 *...Darling Buds of May?*

a9 ...*Upstairs, Downstairs*?

b9 *...The Bill?*

a10 Which daily news programme began in 1967?

b10 *Who was the chief presenter?*

Which ITV television company took over a franchise from...

a11 ...Thames?

b11 *...TVS?*

a12 ...Westward?

b12 *...Television Wales and West?*

No. 83 Answers

a1 'All because the lady loves Milk Tray' (he delivered the box of Cadbury's Milk Tray)

b1 *Birds Eye Fish Fingers*

a2 Heineken

b2 *Hovis*

a3 The Homepride Flour graders

b3 *Dulux Paint*

a4 One of the PG Tips chimps

b4 *Kattomeat*

a5 Schweppes Indian Tonic Water

b5 *Oxo (the Oxo 'family')*

a6 Coca Cola (This was the title of the single they released; in the television commercial they sang 'I'd Like to Buy the World a Coke')

b6 *The New Seekers*

a7 Anglia

b7 *Granada*

a8 ATV and, later, Central

b8 *Yorkshire*

a9 London Weekend

b9 *Thames*

a10 *News At Ten*

b10 *Alastair (later Sir Alastair) Burnett*

a11 Carlton

b11 *Meridian*

a12 TSW (Television South and West)

b12 *Harlech*

Tie-breaker

Q In the Seventies, ITV showed a Saturday morning children's programme called *TISWAS*. For what did T.I.S.W.A.S. stand?

A This Is Saturday Wear a Smile

No. 84 Radio Stars

On radio, for what were the following famous...
a1   ...John Arlott?
b1   ...*Peter Bromley*?
a2   ...Max Jaffa?
b2   ...*Garrison Keillor*?
a3   ...A. J. Alan?
b3   ...*C. H. Middleton*?

Who is chiefly remembered for presenting...
a4   ...*Saturday Club*?
b4   ...*Top Gear*?
a5   ...*In the Psychiatrist's Chair*?
b5   ...*The Food Programme*?
a6   ...*I'm Sorry I Haven't a Clue*?
b6   ...*Just A Minute*?
a7   ...*Brain of Britain*?
b7   ...*My Music*?
a8   ...*Your Hundred Best Tunes*?
b8   ...*The Chapel in the Valley*?

In which radio show did we hear...
a9   ...Jean Metcalfe and Cliff Michelmore?
b9   ...*John Timpson and Jack de Manio*?
a10   ...Uncle Rex, Auntie Elizabeth and Uncle David
b10   ...*Julia Lang and Daphne Oxenford*?
a11   ...Richard Dimbleby, Jack Train and Anona Winn?
b11   ...*Kenneth Horne, Sam Costa and Maurice Denham*?
a12   ...Jimmy Edwards, Ted Ray and Tommy Trinder?
b12   ...*Ralph Wightman, A. G. Street and Mary Stocks*?

No. 84 Answers

a1   Cricket commentaries
b1   *Racing commentaries*
a2   Violinist (leader of the Palm Court Orchestra)
b2   *Tales from Lake Wobegon*
a3   Storytelling (pre-war)
b3   *Gardening advice*
a4   Brian Matthew
b4   *John Peel*
a5   Dr Anthony Clare
b5   *Derek Cooper*
a6   Humphrey Lyttleton
b6   *Nicholas Parsons*
a7   Robert Robinson (originally Franklin Engelmann)
b7   *Steve Race*
a8   Alan Keith
b8   *Sandy Macpherson (the organist)*
a9   *Family Favourites* (later, *Two-Way Family Favourites*)
b9   Today
a10   *Children's Hour*
b10   Listen With Mother
a11   *Twenty Questions*
b11   Much-Binding-in-the-Marsh
a12   *Does the Team Think?*
b12   Any Questions?

Tie-breaker

Q   Who was the first female DJ on Radio One?
A   *Anne (Annie) Nightingale*

No. 85 Get the Guest–5

How many clues do you need before you can identify each of the following stars of the musical? (See page 9)

Guest A
1 Gertrude Lawrence appeared in two of my works; so did Fred Astaire.
2 I collaborated with various composers but especially with my brother.
3 His music struck up the bands on the Broadway stage in the Twenties and Thirties.
4 As for myself, when I say I also got plenty of nothing, it ain't necessarily so.

Guest B
1 During the Twenties I can honestly say I was London's leading lady, certainly so far as operetta was concerned.
2 My last great role was in *Charley Girl* in 1969 but I'd also been *The Belle of New York*.
3 My first husband, Sonnie Hale, later married Jessie Matthews.
4 My greatest role was, however, in *The Merry Widow*.

Guest C
1 I was born in Austria in 1900 but later settled in New York.
2 I became famous for what was once described as my 'steel-like' voice.
3 I appeared in *Cabaret* but am more often linked with Pirate Jenny and Mack the Knife.
4 One of my husband's best-known operas cost only threepence.

Guest D
1 I was born in Cardiff in south Wales and won international fame as a star in silent films.
2 One of my earliest hits was the First World War song, 'Keep the Home Fires Burning'.
3 Since then, I became better known as the writer of romantic musicals.
4 My career took off one glamorous night and my final word was gay.

No. 85 Answers

Guest A
Ira Gershwin (1896–1983)
He was born in New York in 1896, two years before George, with whom he collaborated. Ira's lyrics are noted for their wit and rhyming ingenuity. Gertrude Lawrence appeared in his *Oh, Kay!* (1926) and *Treasure Girl* (1928). Fred Astaire was in *Lady, Be Good!* (1924) and *Funny Face* (1927). Ira Gershwin's show *Strike Up the Band* opened in Broadway in 1930. His songs 'I Got Plenty O' Nothin'' and 'It Ain't Necessarily So' were in *Porgy and Bess* (1935).

Guest B
Evelyn Laye (1900–)
She was born in London in 1900 and was a major star from 1920 onwards, her biggest successes being in *The Shop Girl* (1920), *The Merry Widow* (1923) and *Madame Pompadour* (1923). She appeared in *The Belle of New York* in 1942 and had another great hit in *Wedding in Paris* in 1954. Sonnie Hale was an actor, singer and director, frequently appearing with both Evelyn Laye and Jessie Matthews.

Guest C
Lotte Lenya (1900?–1981)
She was born in Vienna but went to America with her composer-husband Kurt Weill. She appeared in four of his musicals including *Die Dreigroschenoper* ('The Threepenny Opera') in which she sang the number 'Pirate Jenny'. Later she was in the stage version of *Cabaret* and is remembered for her interpretation of Weill's song 'Mack the Knife'.

Guest D
Ivor Novello (1893–1951)
He was born in 1893 and became famous as a composer, lyricist and actor. From 1935, he created a number of operettas: *Glamorous Night* (1935), *Careless Rapture* (1936) and *The Dancing Years* (1939). *Glamorous Night* was his first major triumph; his last show was *Gay's the Word* (1951).

No. 86 Balletomania

In the world of ballet, who...

a1 ...was born on a train in 1938, and escaped from the Soviet Union in 1961?

b1 ...studied dance in Poland, worked with Nijinski and founded her own ballet school in London in 1920?

a2 ..., with Frederick Ashton, danced the roles of the Ugly Sisters in Cinderella?

b2 ...was the dancer, choreographer and director who conceived the musical West Side Story?

By what names do we know the ballerinas...

a3 ...Peggy Hookham?

b3 ...Lilian Alicia Marks?

a4 ...Lynn Springbelt?

b4 ...Edris Stannus?

For what 'job' within the world of dance were the following celebrated...

a5 ...Martha Graham?

b5 ...Serge Diaghilev?

a6 ...Mikhail Fokine?

b6 ...Kenneth MacMillan?

a7 ...Léon Bakst?

b7 ...Anthony Dowell?

What is the meaning of the term...

a8 ...Pas de deux (say: pah de deur)?

b8 ...Pointe (say: pwant) work?

a9 ...Barre?

b9 ...Glissade (say: glee-sarde)?

a10 ...Plié (say: plee-ay)?

b10 ...Entrechat (say: en-tre-shat)?

No. 86 Answers

a1 Rudolf Nureyev
b1 Dame Marie Rambert
a2 Robert Helpmann
b2 Jerome Robbins
a3 Dame Margot Fonteyn
b3 Dame Alicia Markova
a4 Lynn Seymour
b4 Dame Ninette de Valois
a5 Choreographer *or* teacher (of contemporary dance)
b5 Impressario (accept: producer)
a6 Choreographer (also a dancer)
b6 Choreographer or director (originally a dancer)
a7 Designer (provider of décor)
b7 Dancer
a8 Dance for ballerina and her partner
b8 Steps danced on extreme tiptoe
a9 A rail running round the walls of a studio or rehearsal room which dancers hold during exercises
b9 A sliding 'step'
a10 The bending of the knees (e.g. before a jump or on landing); also the first exercise of daily ballet class
b10 A criss-crossing of the legs (before and behind each other) while the dancer is in the air

---

Tie-breaker

Q What is or was a 'balletomane'?
A *An enthusiastic attender at ballets; originally a term used in Russia to mean 'the man who never missed a performance'. In Russia, 'balletomanes' would occupy the best seats and, after the performance, adjourn to a café to meet the dancers and to discuss the performance*

No. 87 Backstage Business

In the theatre, just before the dress rehearsal of a new production there is usually a technical rehearsal–a rehearsal in which all the lighting, sound and other technicians have their last chance to get everything right and the actors are unlikely to get to bed before 2 a.m. It can get a little tense backstage! This round is about 'backstage terms', the technical language of the theatre.

a1   What is Kensington Gore?
b1   *What is a slosh cloth?*
a2   What are barn doors?
b2   *What are dips?*
a3   What is a 'Hamlet wait'?
b3   *What is a Corsican trap?*
a4   What is a DBO?
b4   *What is FUF?*
a5   What is an ASM?
b5   *What is FOH?*
a6   What is 'OP'?
b6   *What is OTT?*

Meanwhile, in the dressing rooms, actors are thinking about their make-up:
a7   What use might burnt cork be to an actor?
b7   *What is 'pancake'?*
a8   What's the meaning of 'Five and nine'?
b8   *What is 'hair lace'?*
a9   What is 'wet white'?
b9   *For what is 'liquid latex' often used?*
a10   When making up, why might you use putty–and how?
b10   *For what purpose did actors once use oatmeal paste?*

No. 87 Answers

a1 Artificial blood

b1 *A stage cloth used to protect the stage during slapstick scenes*

a2 Adjustable metal doors on a lantern, to direct the beam of light

b2 *Small trap doors in the stage, providing access to power sockets*

a3 A prolonged period spent offstage by an actor (like Hamlet's wait off stage between Act IV, scene iii and Act V, scene i)

b3 *A long trap door running across the stage and containing a ramp–often used by 'Ghosts' who can slowly appear up it!*

a4 A 'dead' (i.e. sudden and total) black out

b4 *'Full up to finish.' All the stage lights are brought up to full power during the last few bars of a musical number–to encourage plenty of applause!*

a5 Assistant Stage Manager

b5 *Front of House (the box office, foyer, bars, etc.)*

a6 Opposite Prompt = the opposite side of the stage to where the prompter sits. In Britain this is stage right when you are facing the audience. In the United States it is stage left

b6 *'Over the Top' (exaggerated acting)*

a7 A rough and ready means of 'blacking up' or of suggesting facial hair

b7 *(Non-greasy) make-up base*

a8 They are greasepaint sticks used together to make a (Caucasian) flesh-coloured make-up base

b8 *Flesh-coloured gauze at the front of a wig; used to make hair appear to grow naturally from skin.*

a9 Liquid body make-up (not necessarily white)

b9 *To create a deep scar (Brush the latex on the area to be scarred, let it dry. Squeeze it together to make a crease, then possibly paint it with 'blood')*

a10 For building up false (or extended) noses, etc. ('To remove nose putty, cut away with a cotton thread, as if you were using a cheese wire')

b10 *To remove make-up*

No. 88 Feared by the Bad

A round about television heroes.

a1   Who played Perry Mason?
b1   *And who was 'The Prisoner'?*
a2   Who replaced Roger Moore as Simon Templar?
b2   *In which city does Inspector Taggart operate?*
a3   In *The Avengers,* who played Emma Peel?
b3   *Who played the character she replaced (Catherine Gale)?*
a4   Which long-running police series began life as a 'one off' play called *Woodentop*?
b4   *In Kojak, what was Kojak's first name?*
a5   In which feature film did the character PC George Dixon first appear?
b5   *What happened to him at the end of the film?*
a6   In *The Sweeney,* who played Jack Regan?
b6   *Which character was played by Dennis Waterman?*
a7   For what is 'Sweeney' rhyming slang?
b7   *Garfield Morgan played Chief Inspector...who?*
a8   Who played Haggerty in *Special Branch*?
b8   *And who played Amsterdam detective Van der Valk?*
a9   In which series did Alfred Burke play Frank Marker?
b9   *What was special about the cab service in Rides?*
a10   Which Western series featured Special Agent Jim Hardie?
b10   *Which series about the oil industry featured actor Ray Barrett?*
a11   In which series did Bernard Archer play Colonel Pinto?
b11   *Whom did Bruce Seton play in what was probably the BBC's first crime series?*
a12   In which drama serial did George Withers play a prison governor?
b12   *David McCallum, Jack Hedley and Bernard Hepton starred in which prisoner-of-war series?*

No. 88 Answers

a1 Raymond Burr
b1 *Patrick McGoohan (in* The Prisoner*)*
a2 Ian Ogilvy (in *Return of the Saint*)
b2 *Glasgow*
a3 Diana Rigg
b3 *Honor Blackman*
a4 *The Bill*
b4 *Theo*
a5 *The Blue Lamp*
b5 *He was shot dead (by a young criminal–played by Dirk Bogarde)*
a6 John Thaw
b6 *Sergeant Carter*
a7 The Flying Squad ('Sweeney Todd–the Flying Squad')
b7 *Haskins*
a8 Patrick Mower
b8 *Barry Foster*
a9 *Public Eye*
b9 *It was run by and for women*
a10 *Wells Fargo*
b10 The Troubleshooters
a11 *Spycatcher*
b11 *Detective Superintendent Fabian (in* Fabian of the Yard*)*
a12 *Within These Walls*
b12 Colditz

Tie-breaker

Q Which show began: 'The story you are about to see is true, only
the names have been changed to protect the innocent'?
A Dragnet *(made in America, shown on ITV)*

No. 89 Early Greats

A round featuring 8 of the greatest films ever made–and the most recent dates from 1942. Can you say which film is being described–and fill in the missing name in each description?

a1 A magazine reporter 'interviews the friends of a dead newspaper tycoon (who was played by the film's director _____) in order to discover the meaning of his dying word, 'Rosebud'

b1 The path of true love is thwarted by mistaken identity but is helped by show-stopping numbers such as 'Cheek to Cheek' –with the character Dale Tremont sung and danced by _____

a2 Despite music and sound effects, it was in effect a silent movie released in the fifth year of the sound era. It is about a tramp (played by the film's director _____) who meets a millionaire and falls in love with a blind flower-seller

b2 One of the first 'talkies' to be made in Britain, it is about a Scotland Yard inspector who finds his girlfriend is involved in a murder. He keeps quiet about the fact–with results that give the film its title. Even in this 1929 film, the director _____ himself appears in a cameo role

a3 An old-fashioned professor becomes infatuated by a night club singer, a role created by _____–whose career was 'made' by this 1930 film which was shot in both German and in English

b3 Rick's Café is a centre for war refugees, a night club presided over by the cynical Rick and into which walks his one-time love (played by _____) who asks the pianist to play a certain tune and Rick to get her two visas

a4 A 1915 silent film which is irredeemably racist (and pro-Ku Klux Klan) but which was nevertheless a milestone in cinema history with its use of close-ups, flashbacks and battle scenes–all created by its director _____

b4 Issued in 1924 as a silent movie and re-issued in 1942 with music and narration, this film tells the story of a 'little tramp' character trying to survive in the frozen wastes of Alaska–even to the extent of eating his _____

No. 89 Answers

a1   *Citizen Kane*;
Orson Welles

b1   Top Hat*;
Ginger Rogers (her co-star was, of course, Fred Astaire)

a2   *City Lights*;
Charlie Chaplin

b2   Blackmail*;
Alfred Hitchcock

a3   *The Blue Angel* (*Der Blaue Engel*);
Marlene Dietrich

b3   Casablanca*;
Ingrid Bergman (the tune is 'As Time Goes By' and Rick is played by Humphrey Bogart)

a4   *The Birth of a Nation*;
D. W. Griffith

b4   The Gold Rush*;
boots

Tie-breaker

Q Which 1932 movie (starring Greta Garbo, Joan Crawford and John Barrymore) was re-made in 1945 as *Weekend at the Waldorf*?

A Grand Hotel

No. 90 Dramatis Personae–3

In which play or musical would you encounter the following characters?

a1   Olga, Masha and Irina?
b1   *Donna Lucia from Brazil?*
a2   Gary Essendine?
b2   *Mr and Mrs Dung Beetle?*
a3   Dol Common and Sir Epicure Mammon?
b3   *Mickey and Edward (they're brothers)?*
a4   Mrs Elvsted?
b4   *Roy Cohn?*
a5   Dull and Costard?
b5   *Georges et Albin?*
a6   St John Quatermaine?
b6   *Movie journalist Allan Felix?*
a7   Green Eyes, Maurice and Lefranc?
b7   *Captain Shotover and Mazzini Dunn?*
a8   Billy Fisher?
b8   *Big Daddie?*
a9   Hally, Sam and Willie?
b9   *Shelley Levene and Richard Roma?*
a10   Frederic, the pirate apprentice?
b10   *Ko-Ko and Pooh-Bah?*
a11   Goldberg and Meg?
b11   *Jimmy and Alison?*
a12   Mollie and Giles Ralston?
b12   *Willie Mossup, Alice and Maggie?*

No. 90 Answers

a1 *Three Sisters* by Anton Chekhov
b1 Charley's Aunt *by Brandon Thomas*
a2 *Present Laughter* by Noël Coward
b2 The Insect Play *by Karel and Josef Capek (sometimes known as 'The Insect Comedy')*
a3 *The Alchemist* by Ben Jonson
b3 Blood Brothers *by Willy Russell*
a4 *Hedda Gabler* by Henrik Ibsen
b4 Angels in America *by Tony Kushner*
a5 *Love's Labour's Lost* by Shakespeare
b5 La Cage Aux Folles *by Harvey Fierstein*
a6 *Quatermaine's Terms* by Simon Gray
b6 Play It Again, Sam *by Woody Allen*
a7 *Deathwatch* by Jean Genet
b7 Heartbreak House *by Bernard Shaw*
a8 *Billy Liar* by Keith Waterhouse and Willis Hall
b8 Cat On a Hot Tin Roof *by Tennessee Williams*
a9 *'Master Harold'...and the Boys* by Athol Fugard
b9 Glengarry Glen Ross *by David Mamet*
a10 *The Pirates of Penzance* by Gilbert and Sullivan
b10 The Mikado *by Gilbert and Sullivan*
a11 *The Birthday Party* by Harold Pinter
b11 Look Back in Anger *by John Osborne*
a12 *The Mousetrap* by Agatha Christie
b12 Hobson's Choice *by Harold Brighouse*

Tie-breaker

Q Which of John Godber's plays is about a group of young people on a skiing holiday?
A On the Piste

No. 91 Into the Nineties

A round of questions about films which were on release in the early Nineties.

a1   In which 1993 film did things go wrong on Isla Nublar?
b1   *Who played the owner of the park on that island?*
a2   Which film studio 'shrunk the kids'?
b2   *Which 1991 film from the same studio starred a teapot, a candelabra and a clock?*
a3   Which child actor was left 'Home Alone'?
b3   *What was the full title of the sequel to this film?*

Who played...
a4   ...Hannibal Lecter in *The Silence of the Lambs*?
b4   *...Batman in* Batman*?*
a5   ...a Union Officer who chose to live with Sioux Indians (in *Dances with Wolves*)?
b5   *...Michael Corleone (the Godfather's son) in* The Godfather Part III*?*
a6   ...breathless Mahoney in *Dick Tracy*?
b6   *...Miss Daisy in* Driving Miss Daisy*?*
a7   ...the cabaret singer in *The Fabulous Baker Boys*?
b7   *...the fictional action man in* Last Action Hero*?*
a8   ...the disabled Vietnam veteran in *Born on the Fourth of July*?
b8   *...a millionaire who hires an escort in* Pretty Woman*?*
a9   Who was the star of the 1992 Oscar-winning picture *Unforgiven*?
b9   *Which comic fantasy was about a TV weatherman 'getting his girl'–and a lot of snow?*
a10   Which Black Power leader was played by Denzel Washington?
b10   *Which 1990 film, set in 2084, was based on a science fiction story by Philip K. Dick?*
a11   Which Shakespearian leading character did Mel Gibson play?
b11   *Who created the film?*
a12   On which Shakespearian play was *Prospero's Books* based?
b12   *Who played Prospero?*

No. 91 Answers

a1 *Jurassic Park*
b1 *Richard Attenborough*
a2 Walt Disney (the film was *Honey I Shrunk the Kids*)
b2 Beauty and the Beast
a3 Macaulay Culkin
b3 Home Alone 2–Lost in New York
a4 Anthony Hopkins
b4 *Michael Keaton*
a5 Kevin Costner
b5 *Al Pacino*
a6 Madonna
b6 *Jessica Tandy*
a7 Michelle Pfeiffer
b7 *Arnold Schwarzenegger*
a8 Tom Cruise
b8 *Richard Gere*
a9 Clint Eastwood
b9 Groundhog Day
a10 Malcolm X (in *Malcolm X*)
b10 Total Recall
a11 Hamlet
b11 *Franco Zeffirelli*
a12 *The Tempest*
b12 *Sir John Gielgud*

Tie-breaker

Q Name the four baby turtles that fall into a New York sewer in *Teenage Mutant Ninja Turtles*–and the ninja-master who teaches them the martial arts

A *Raphael, Michelangelo, Donatello and Leonardo; and Splinter*

No. 92 Hidden Titles–10

Within each of these dialogues are hidden eight play titles. Can you spot the titles and say who is the author of each group?

Team A

(*An upper-class young man and his fiancée are house-hunting*)

She This place. It's far too small. Just a doll's house. *And* it's full of ghosts.

He My little duckling, it's modern. Architect designed. Put up by a master builder.

She Oh that man. Lord Gynt.

He He's a peer of the realm. He's one of the pillars of society.

She More like an enemy of the people. I'd like to brand him for what he is. Look, we ought to wake up, we, the people who have to live in these places. When we dead awaken–

He You're talking wild nonsense, wild, duckling, wild, I say.

Team B

(*He is respectful; she is his social 'superior'–but she is also gracious*)

She It's good to meet you again, Master Harold. And the boys as well, hello!

He Good afternoon, m' lady. (*Mutterings from the boys?*) But you're not with your faithful companion. What was his name? Sizwe?

She Bansi. Is dead. He died in an accident on the road to Mecca.

He Oh, an accident! Was there much blood?

She Blood? Not much.

He And where do you live now, ma'am?

She On the island.

He The island!

She People *are* living there now, you know. So, we'll meet again.

He What about Friday?

She No good. Friday...no good. Another time.

He So it's hello and goodbye.

She (*Putting him down finally*) Yes.

195

No. 92 Answers

Team A titles

A Doll's House
Ghosts
The Master Builder
Pillars of Society
An Enemy of the People
Brand
When We Dead Awaken
The Wild Duck
and their author is the Norwegian playwright, Henrik Ibsen

Team B titles

Master Harold and the Boys
Sizwe Bansi Is Dead
The Road to Mecca
Blood Knot
The Island
People Are Living There
No Good Friday
Hello and Goodbye
and their author is the South African playwright, Athol Fugard

No. 93 Soap on the Box–2

a1 Which soap character was famous for his woolly hat?

b1 *And which one was famous for her hairnet?*

a2 In *Neighbours*, which character did Jason Donovan play?

b2 *And which did Kylie Minogue play?*

a3 In 1981, who married Deirdre Langton?

b3 *Two years later, with whom did she have an affair?*

a4 Which ward was under the control of Sister Carole Young?

b4 *Which of its doctors was played by Desmond Carrington?*

And now some soap 'deaths'...

a5 ...how did Jack Sugden's wife Pat die?

b5 *...who shot J. R.?*

a6 ...how and where did Ernest Bishop die?

b6 *...and how did baby Hassan Osman die?*

a7 To which country did Elsie Tanner move with Bill Gregory when she left 'the Street'?

b7 *And to which country did Meg Mortimer sail away when she was written out of* Crossroads?

a8 Which 1965 soap was about a family who had moved into an East Anglian overspill town?

b8 *Who played their neighbour and (later) EastEnders' Pauline?*

a9 Which brewery supplies the Rover's Return?

b9 *And which real ale is on sale in* Emmerdale Farm's *Woolpack?*

a10 Who wrote the theme tune for *Neighbours*?

b10 *And who wrote the* Coronation Street *theme?*

a11 Who created *Coronation Street*?

b11 *And who created* Crossroads?

a12 In the 'spoof' soap opera *Acorn Antiques*, who played plump Miss Bertie (and wrote the scripts)?

b12 *And who played the baggy-stockinged char, Mrs Overall?*

No. 93 Answers

a1 Benny Hawkins (*Crossroads*)
b1 *Ena Sharples (Coronation Street)*
a2 Scott Robinson
b2 *Charlene Mitchell*
a3 Ken Barlow
b3 *Mike Baldwin*
a4 Ward 10 (in *Emergency–Ward 10*)
b4 *Dr (Chris) Anderson*
a5 In a hit-and-run road accident (in *Emmerdale Farm*)
b5 *Kristin (Sue Ellen's sister) (in Dallas)*
a6 Shot in a raid on Mike Baldwin's factory (in *Coronation Street*)
b6 *Cot death (in* EastEnders' *first year)*
a7 Portugal
b7 *New York*
a8 *The Newcomers*
b8 *Wendy Richards*
a9 Newton and Ridley
b9 *Efram Monks*
a10 Tony Hatch
b10 *Eric Spear*
a11 Tony Warren
b11 *Hazel Adair and Peter Ling (its first producer was Reg Watson)*
a12 Victoria Wood
b12 *Julie Walters*

Tie-breaker

Q Who was the only member of the original cast of *Crossroads* to stay with the show till its end?

A *Jane Rossington (who played Jill Richardson, later Jill Crane, Jill Harvey, Jill Chance, Jill Maddingham)*

No. 94 Off the Set

Quite often, 'showbiz' personalities have to live their private lives in public–including personal tragedies.

Can you identify the following...?

a1   ...born Eric Bartholomew, he was awarded the OBE in 1976 and died of a heart attack in 1984

b1   ...She was born in 1959, brought up a Catholic and has become known for her raunchy book, film and pop records. Who is she?

a2   ...a Liverpool comedian, he appeared in court as a result of his dealings with the Inland Revenue

b2   *...a stand-up (or sit-down) comic, he used to smoke Gauloise cigarettes and lost half of the first finger on his left hand in a car door accident*

a3   ...one of the comedy group *The Goodies*, he is (in real life) a doctor of medicine

b3   *...another member of the group, he is a keen ornithologist*

a4   ...known as the 'Big Yin', he flew to Mozambique in 1989 to help Comic Relief

b4   *...The Sun newspaper ran a headline in 1986 about him eating a hamster*

a5   ...a *What's My Line?* panelist, she committed suicide after being accused of shop-lifting

b5   *...another panelist on that show, he was somewhat irascible and had a drink problem*

a6   Where did the actor Leonard Rossiter die (he played Rigsby and Reginald Perrin on television)?

b6   *Where did the comedian Tony Hancock die?*

a7   Back in the Fifties, which Oscar-winning film star married Carlo Ponti?

b7   *Which very famous film star was found dead and naked in August 1962?*

a8   Which comic actor married actress Britt Ekland in 1964?

b8   *To which film director was actress Amy Irving married until 1989?*

No. 94 Answers

a1   Eric Morecambe
b1   *Madonna*
a2   Ken Dodd
b2   *Dave Allen*
a3   Graeme Garden
b3   *Bill Oddie*
a4   Billy Connolly
b4   *Freddie Starr ('Freddie Starr Ate My Hamster'; he denied the story)*
a5   Lady Isobel Barnet
b5   *Gilbert Harding*
a6   Backstage in a London theatre (during the interval of a play in which he was appearing–it was Joe Orton's black comedy about a dead body, *Loot*)
b6   *In an Australian hotel room (he committed suicide)*
a7   Sophia Loren
b7   *Marilyn Monroe*
a8   Peter Sellers
b8   *Steven Spielberg*

Tie-breaker

Q   Whose 40th birthday party (in 1972) was attended by Ringo Starr and Princess Grace of Monaco–while her husband gave her a $50,000 diamond pendant?

A   *Elizabeth Taylor*

No. 95 A Night at the Opera

Opera glasses ready: can you say in which opera we can see (and hear) these characters—and who composed each work?

a1   Figaro, Count Almaviva and Susanna?
b1   *Figaro, Count Almaviva and Rosina?*
a2   Papageno, a bird-catcher?
b2   *A duke's jester who is also a hunchback?*
a3   Iago and Desdemona?
b3   *Mephistopheles and Marguerite?*
a4   A chorus of cigarette girls?
b4   *A chorus of fisherfolk in an East Anglian town?*
a5   A famous singer, a painter and the chief of police?
b5   *Ping, Pong and Pang?*
a6   Leonore (or Leonora), Don Fernando and Florestan?
b6   *Clorinda, Tisbe, Angelina and Prince Ramiro?*
a7   Manrico, Azucena (a gypsy) and Leonora?
b7   *Venus, goddess of love, and Wolfram, a knight?*
a8   Lieutenant B. F. Pinkerton?
b8   *Herod and Herodias?*
a9   Donna Elvira, Donna Anna and Leporello?
b9   *Tatyana, her sister Olga and Vladimir Lensky?*
a10   Violetta, a courtesan?
b10   *Captain Vere and other sailors?*
a11   Edgar (Master of Ravenswood) and Lucy?
b11   *The high priest and the King of Egypt?*
a12   Mimi, Marcello (a painter) and Rodolfo (a poet)?
b12   *Jenik, Marenta and Bohemian villagers?*

No. 95 Answers

a1 *The Marriage of Figaro (Le Nozze di Figaro)* by Mozart
b1 The Barber of Seville *(Il Barbiere di Siviglia) by Rossini*
a2 *The Magic Flute (Die Zauberflöte)* by Mozart
b2 Rigoletto *by Verdi: (the jester is Rigoletto himself)*
a3 *Otello (Othello)* by Verdi
b3 Faust *by Gounod*
a4 *Carmen* by Bizet
b4 Peter Grimes *by (Benjamin) Britten*
a5 *Tosca* by Puccini (Tosca, Cavaradossi and Baron Scarpia)
b5 Turandot *by Puccini (the Grand Chancellor, the General Purveyor and the Chief Cook: three of Turandot's ministers)*
a6 *Fidelio* by Beethoven
b6 Cinderella *(La Cenerentola) by Rossini*
a7 *Il Trovatore (The Troubadour)* by Verdi
b7 Tannhäuser *by Wagner*
a8 *Madame Butterfly* by Puccini
b8 Salomé *by (Richard) Strauss*
a9 *Don Giovanni (Don Juan)* by Mozart
b9 Eugene Onegin *by Tchaikovsky*
a10 *La Traviata (The Woman Gone Astray)* by Verdi
b10 Billy Budd *by (Benjamin) Britten*
a11 *Lucia di Lammermoor (Lucy of Lammermoor)* by Donizetti
b11 Aida *by Verdi*
a12 *La Bohème (Bohemian Life)* by Puccini
b12 The Battered Bride *(Prodaná Nevèsta) by Smetana*

Tie-breaker

Q In which opera are there a goldsmith, a cobbler, a furrier, a tin-smith, a baker, a soap-boiler, a pewterer, a tailor, a grower, a coppersmith and a stocking-weaver?

A Die Meistersinger von Nuremberg *(They are the 'Mastersingers' in Wagner's opera,* The Mastersingers of Nuremberg*)*

No. 96 More Great Titles

A second round of film titles for you to complete. Like Quiz No. 46, this could be a 'speed' round in which you see who (or which team) can answer first

a1 *The Lavender Hill...?*
b1 Pennies from...?
a2 *The Man Who Shot...?*
b2 The Man Who Fell...?
a3 *Love Me...?*
b3 Love on the...?
a4 *Mourning Becomes...?*
b4 Long Day's...?
a5 *The Maltese...?*
b5 The Manchurian...?
a6 *No Way to...?*
b6 On a Clear Day...?
a7 *The Postman...?*
b7 The Silence of...?
a8 *McCabe and...?*
b8 She Wore a...?
a9 *Please Don't...?*
b9 Teahouse of...?
a10 *Sands of...?*
b10 They Shoot...?
a11 *Will Success...?*
b11 Whistle Down...?
a12 *The Quiller...?*
b12 The Pumpkin...?

No. 96 Answers

a1 *Mob*
b1 Heaven
a2 *Liberty Valance*
b2 to Earth
a3 *Tender* or *Tonight* or *or Leave Me*
b3 Dole *or* Run
a4 *Electra*
b4 Journey into Night or Long Day's Dying
a5 *Falcon*
b5 Candidate
a6 *Treat a Lady*
b6 You Can See Forever
a7 *Always Rings Twice*
b7 the Lambs
a8 *Mrs Miller*
b8 Yellow Ribbon
a9 *Eat the Daisies*
b9 the August Moon
a10 *Iwo Jima*
b10 Horses, Don't They?
a11 *Spoil Rock Hunter?*
b11 the Wind
a12 *Memorandum*
b12 Eater

Tie-breaker

Q Which film titles can you think of that begin with the word 'Midnight'?

A Midnight *(there were two films with this title)*, Midnight Angel, Midnight Club, Midnight Cowboy, Midnight Episode, Midnight Express, Midnight Lace, Midnight Madonna, Midnight Mary, Midnight Patrol, Midnight Taxi *(and also* The Midnight Men)

No. 97 The Number One Tour

In this round, we undertake an international Number One Tour, playing in four famous theatres. In which towns or cities will we be playing? (Teams could win more points the more quickly they can say where they'll be performing.) And, as a clue, on this tour we are travelling round the world eastwards.

Team A
We opened in...
1 Its theatre was badly bombed in 1943 but beautifully restored.
2 The building was started in 1776 and completed two years later.
3 It has no 'circle' or gallery but six tiers of boxes stretch right around the auditorium.
4 It's often been described as the 'Queen of Opera Houses'.

Team B
Then we played...
1 This building has some of the very best acoustics of any theatre.
2 Its best surviving feature is its orchestra.
3 It seats approximately 14,000 people–in the open air.
4 It was first used about 350 BC.

Team A
A week later we did the show in...
1 The city it's in is famous for amateur theatre: it is said to have 3,000 registered amateur companies.
2 The theatre is called The Star and is the base of The Star Theatre Company.
3 The city has a film industry, but not as thriving a one as its west-coast rival.

Team B
Finally, we closed in...
1 This building was designed by a Dane, Jørn Utzon.
2 It contains five auditoria, 50 dressing rooms and two rehearsal rooms.
3 Situated on Bennelong Point, it looks like a series of interlocking shells.

No. 97 Answers

Team A
We opened in...
Milan in Italy (Teatro alla Scala–'La Scala')

Team B
Then we played...
Epidauros (or Epidavros or Επιδαυρος) near Athens in Greece. *NB* The 'orchestra' is the round 'dancing floor' used by the Chorus (who commentate on the action in a Greek tragedy) in front of the *skene*, or stage proper

Team A
A week later we did the show in...
Calcutta (The Star Theatre), in India. *NB* Calcutta's 'west-coast rival' is Bombay, the centre of the Indian film industry

Team B
Finally, we closed in...
Sydney Opera House in Australia

Tie-breaker

Q Can you identify this location from these three clues, and say which Shakespeare play is set there?
(1) What should anyone do in this place?
(2) One might not without danger walk these streets
   If once, in a sea-fight one did some service...
(3) A noble duke, in nature as in name, governs here

A *Illyria (in heaven knows which country) in* Twelfth Night
(1) 'What should I do in Illyria?' asks Viola on her arrival there;
(2) Antonio speaks in these terms to Sebastian and (3) the sea captain says this to Viola

---

No. 98 Drama on the Box

Which television drama series was about...

a1 ...a group of women interned by the Japanese during the Second World War?

b1 ...a gang of 'Geordie' brickies working in Germany?

a2 ...the inmates of an Australian women's prison?

b2 ...the regulars in a Boston bar?

a3 ...an American inner-city police precinct and a lawyer called Joyce Davenport?

b3 ...a London CID officer called Maggie Forbes?

In which series did...

a4 ...Terence Alexander play a policeman's ex-father-in-law?

b4 ...Stephanie Turner play Detective Inspector Jean Darblay?

a5 ...Peter Bowles and Bryan Murray play two conmen?

b5 ...Clive Owen play business analyst Steven Crane?

a6 ...Dennis Waterman play a self-made man, uncertain how to cope with wealth and servants?

b6 ...James Bolam and Lynda Bellingham play two divorcees?

a7 ...Keith Barron play a drinking, wenching 18th-century squire?

b7 ...Penelope Keith play a Labour MP?

a8 Which drama serial followed the Ashtons during the Second World War?

b8 Which 1961 series was about 'all the life and loves of a big London department store'?

a9 Which television drama gave us the phrase 'Gissa job'?

b9 Which character repeatedly said it?

a10 Who played the role?

b10 Who wrote the serial?

a11 Who was the star of the drama serial Edge of Darkness?

b11 Who wrote it (he also created Z-Cars)?

a12 Which actor shocked viewers by playing a naked (in some scenes!) Lake District bank manager?

b12 This was a serial called A Time To Dance. Who wrote the novel on which it was based?

No. 98 Answers

a1 *Tenko*
b1 *Auf Wiedersehen Pet*
a2 *Prisoner Cell Block H*
b2 Cheers
a3 *Hill Street Blues*
b3 The Gentle Touch
a4 *Bergerac* (Charlie Hungerford)
b4 Juliet Bravo
a5 *(The) Perfect Scoundrels*
b5 Chancer
a6 *On the Up*
b6 Second Thoughts
a7 *Haggard*
b7 No Job for a Lady
a8 *A Family at War*
b8 Harpers West One
a9 *Boys from the Blackstuff*
b9 *Yosser*
a10 Bernard Hill
b10 *Alan Bleasdale*
a11 Bob Peck
b11 *Troy Kennedy Martin*
a12 Ronald Pickup
b12 *Melvyn Bragg*

Tie-breaker

Q Who played the 'Gold Blend' couple in the coffee commercials?
A *Anthony Head and Sharon Maughan*

No. 99 Odd One Out–3

Team A

Here are three speeches which sound as if they might have been written by Harold Pinter–but only two are genuine. Which is the impostor, and do you know where the true ones come from?

Pinter Speech 1

Trouble is, it ain't easy reaching Bolsover Street. Not on account of the one-way system. What you got to do is, see, is go *down* Titchfield Street, past where you'd turn right to go to the George, but take the next right, then keep going straight across the main road, round the square keeping to the outside lane, then you find yourself at a pedestrian crossing. (*Thoughtful*) There's always the same old woman there... (*Resuming*) Anyway, you takes the next left, then a right and left again and all you got to do is go through three more sets of lights, turn right and left again and that's Bolsover Street. My uncle used to live there.

Pinter Speech 2

It turned out he was born in the Caledonian Road, just before you get to the Nag's Head. His old mum was still living at the Angel. All the buses passed right by the door. She could get a 38, 581, 30 or 38A, take her down the Essex Road to Dalston Junction in next to no time. Well, of course, if she got the 30 he'd take her up Upper Street way, round by Highbury Corner and down to St Paul's Church, but she'd get to Dalston Junction just the same in the end. I used to leave my bike in her garden on my way to work.

Pinter Speech 3

I see you talking to two strangers as I come in. You want to stop talking to strangers, old piece of boot like you, you mind who you talk to. (*Pause*) That's another all-night bus gone down. (*Pause*) Going up the other way. Fulham way. (*Pause*) You ever been down the other way? That was a two-nine-seven. (*Pause*) I've never been up that way. I've been down to Liverpool Street. (*Pause*) I don't fancy going down there, down Fulham way, and all up there.

Team B

Here are three speeches which might or might not have been written by Samuel Beckett. Which is the impostor–and from which plays do the other two come?

Beckett Speech 1

I must have tried. I *have* tried, haven't I? Say yes. Say YES. (*Pause*) (*Sighs*) No matter. Case the heart in steel and polish it with sweat. (*Pause*) Why doesn't time pass? I used to think there was a difference between one fraction of a minute and the next. One fraction of a second and the next. But I don't protest any more. The wind stirs the trees and we're waiting here.

Beckett Speech 2

I once knew a madman who thought the end of the world had come. He was a painter–and engraver. I used to go and see him, in the asylum. I'd take him by the hand and drag him to the window. Look! There! All that rising corn! And there! Look! The sails of the herring fleet! All that loveliness! He'd snatch his hand away and go back into his corner. Appalled. All he had seen was ashes.

Beckett Speech 3

I must be getting on. Thank you for your society. Unless I smoke another pipe before I go. What do you say? Oh I'm only a small smoker, a very small smoker, I'm not in the habit of smoking two pipes one on top of another, it makes my heart go pit-a-pat. It's the nicotine, one absorbs it in spite of one's precautions. You know how it is? But perhaps you don't smoke?

(Answers on page 255)

No. 100 Where's That From?–4

From which theatrical classic does each of the following come–and which character speaks the line?

a1 'The barge she sat, like a burnish'd throne
Burn'd on the water...'

b1 *'Lady Teazle by all that's wonderful.'*

a2 'How grateful we were to the BBC in those dark days of the war when every night at nine o'clock Alvar Lidell brought us news of fresh disasters.'

b2 *'I wonder that you still be talking, Signior Benedick: nobody marks you.'*

a3 'Why, this is hell, nor am I out of it.'

b3 *'No cucumbers!' 'No sir. Not even for ready money.'*

a4 'Big Daddy hadn't been at the table two minutes with those five no-neck monsters slobbering and drooling over their food before he threw down his fork and shouted, "For God's sake Cooper, why don't you put those pigs at the trough?" '

b4 *'The sheep I shall swaddle up in this shawl,
And lie me down straight here beside the wall.'*

a5 'Do you see yonder cloud that's almost in shape of a camel?'

b5 *'I cannon off the middle cushion! I pot into the middle pocket.'*

a6 'I had a sudden presentiment that I was going to have a puncture so I went back to fetch my pump.'

b6 *'Why do I do this every Sunday? Even the book reviews seem to be the same as last week's.'*

a7 'Reputation, reputation, reputation! O! I have lost my reputation...'

b7 *'You didn't mention an acrobat? Or a naked woman swinging from the chandeliers?'*

a8 'If you have tears, prepare to shed them now.'

b8 *'A nose–ah yes, a nose enough!
On seeing it, one thinks "It can't be true!" '*

No. 100 Answers

a1   Enobarbus in *Antony and Cleopatra* by Shakespeare
b1   *Sir Peter Teazle in* The School for Scandal *by R. B. Sheridan*
a2   Dudley Moore in the revue *Beyond the Fringe*
b2   *Beatrice in* Much Ado About Nothing *by Shakespeare*
a3   Mephistophilis in *Doctor Faustus* by Marlowe
b3   *Algernon (Algy) and Lane in* The Importance of Being Earnest *by Oscar Wilde*
a4   Margaret in *Cat On a Hot Tin Roof* by Tennessee Williams
b4   *Mak the sheep stealer in the medieval* Wakefield Shepherds' Play
a5   Hamlet (to Polonius) in *Hamlet* by Shakespeare
b5   *Gayev in* The Cherry Orchard *by Chekhov*
a6   Madame Arcati in *Blithe Spirit* by Noël Coward
b6   *Jimmy Porter at the start of* Look Back in Anger *by John Osborne*
a7   Cassio (to Iago) in *Othello* by Shakespeare
b7   *Inspector Bones (to George) in* Jumpers *by Tom Stoppard*
a8   Mark Antony in *Julius Caesar* by Shakespeare
b8   *Ragueneau in Edmond Rostand's* Cyrano de Bergerac

Tie-breaker

Q Which comic actor spoke these lines (originally on a radio programme and later on a record)?:
'This is busy High Street, focal point of the town's activities. Note the quaint old stores whose frontage is covered with hand-painted inscriptions, every one a rare example of native Balham art.'
A *Peter Sellers*

No. 101 Mr Director

Who directed these films:

a1 *Oh! What a Lovely War, Gandhi* and *Cry Freedom?*
b1 Samson and Delilah, The Greatest Show on Earth *and* The Ten Commandments*?*
a2 *Straw Dogs, The Wild Bunch* and *The Getaway?*
b2 Oklahoma!, High Noon *and* From Here to Eternity*?*
a3 *Lawrence of Arabia, Brief Encounter* and *Ryan's Daughter?*
b3 Midnight Cowboy, A Kind of Loving *and* Darling*?*
a4 *Chimes at Midnight, Citizen Kane* and *Othello?*
b4 The Music Lovers, The Boy Friend *and* Lisztomania*?*
a5 *Anatomy of a Murder, Advise and Consent* and *Exodus?*
b5 Double Indemnity, Some Like It Hot *and* Sunset Boulevard*?*
a6 *The Third Man, Our Man in Havana* and *Oliver!?*
b6 The Muppet Movie, Fraggle Rock *and* The Storyteller*?*
a7 *The Servant, Accident* and *The Go-Between?*
b7 A Clockwork Orange, Lolita *and* 2001: A Space Odyssey*?*
a8 *Romeo and Juliet, Jesus of Nazareth* and *The Taming of the Shrew?*
b8 Babes in Arms, Strike Up the Band *and* For Me and My Girl*?*
a9 *The Maltese Falcon, Key Largo* and *The African Queen?*
b9 Rosemary's Baby, Macbeth *and* Tess*?*
a10 *Cries and Whispers, The Seventh Seal* and *Fanny and Alexander?*
b10 Mon Oncle, Monsieur Hulot's Holiday *and* Traffic*?*
a11 *La Dolce Vita, 8½* and *Ginger and Fred?*
b11 Arsenic and Old Lace, It Happened One Night *and* You Can't Take It With You*?*
a12 *A Bout de Souffle* (*Breathless*) and *Nouvelle Vague?*
b12 Belle de Jour *and* The Discreet Charm of the Bourgeoisie*?*

No. 101 Answers

a1 Richard Attenborough
b1 *Cecil B. De Mille*
a2 Sam Peckinpah
b2 *Fred Zinnemann*
a3 David Lean
b3 *John Schlesinger*
a4 Orson Welles
b4 *Ken Russell*
a5 Otto Preminger
b5 *Billy Wilder*
a6 Carol Reed
b6 *Jim Henson*
a7 Joseph Losey
b7 *Stanley Kubrick*
a8 Franco Zeffirelli
b8 *Busby Berkeley*
a9 John Huston
b9 *Roman Polanski*
a10 Ingmar Bergman
b10 *Jacques Tati*
a11 Federico Fellini
b11 *Frank Capra*
a12 Jean-Luc Godard
b12 *Luis Buñuel*

Tie-breaker

Q Which code (which became compulsory in 1943) set rules for American films such as how long a kiss could last, and permitted physical contact only so long as both pairs of feet were kept on the ground?

A *The Hays Code (it was abandoned in 1968)*

No. 102 Hidden Titles–11

Within each of these dialogues are hidden the titles of eight modern plays. Can you spot the titles and say who wrote each play?

Team A

He Where on earth are you?

She At the kitchen sink, where do you expect?

He Oh look at the mess. We live like pigs in all this squalor.

She Your mother's bizarre habits weren't any better.

He You leave the sport of my–

She –Mad–

He –mother out of it. We're talking about all *this*. That's irrelevant. Inadmissible evidence.

She Calm down. There's no need to look back in anger at the past.

He So what are we having for supper?

She Chicken soup. With barley and vegetable roots and whatever I can find.

He Just vegetables?

She I'm not talking about ordinary vegetables. I'm talking about Jerusalem artichokes.

Team B

He So you've decided where we're going for the visit?

She Sit down on one of the chairs and I'll explain.

He I feel like part of the audience.

She So what we'll–

He It'll be a real holiday?

She You'll have no cares at all. You'll be a traveller without luggage, sunning yourself on the balcony with the maids to do all the work.

He Are you...are you sure?

She Yes.

He And can we go to Spain?

She (*Worried*) Not for the bullfighting?

He It's an art. Magic. (*Getting carried away*) The polka of the picadors, the mamba of the matadors, the waltz of the toreadors...

No. 102 Answers

Team A plays
The Kitchen by Arnold Wesker
Live Like Pigs by John Arden
The Sport of My Mad Mother by Ann Jellicoe
Inadmissible Evidence by John Osborne
Look Back in Anger by John Osborne
Chicken Soup with Barley by Arnold Wesker
Roots by Arnold Wesker
I'm Talking About Jerusalem by Arnold Wesker

Team B plays
The Visit by Friedrich Dürrenmatt
The Chairs by Eugene Ionesco
The Audience by Vaclav Havel
Traveller Without Luggage by Jean Anouilh
The Balcony by Jean Genet
The Maids by Jean Genet
R.U.R. (Rossum's Universal Robots) by Karel Capek
The Waltz of the Toreadors by Jean Anouilh

No. 103 Vintage Comedy...

...on the small screen.

a1   Who were the two stars of *Happy Ever After*?

b1   *The series was later called...what?*

a2   *Grace and Favour* reunited the cast of which earlier 'sit com'?

b2   *Who was comedian Arthur Haynes' 'straight man'?*

a3   Who played the male lead in the serial *A Bit of a Do*?

b3   *In which comedy did Paul Nicholas and Jan Francis play Vince and Penny?*

a4   Which series was about a teacher joining a 'Singles' club?

b4   *Which series was set in the Bayview Retirement Village?*

a5   Who closed their show by saying 'It's goodbye from me'–'And it's goodbye from him'?

b5   *Who played 'The Two Rons'?*

a6   In which comedy series did Wendy Craig play Jennifer?

b6   *And in which series was Derek Nimmo an ineffectual curate?*

a7   To which series was *In Sickness and In Health* a follow-up?

b7   *Of which imaginary school was Jimmy Edwards the headmaster in Whack-O!?*

a8   Which comedy show featured Hut 29 and CSM Bullimore?

b8   *Which two characters from the show got their own series?*

a9   Who played Dad in *The Fosters*?

b9   *Which 17-year-old played their son Sonny?*

a10   Which comedy show was about a package holiday in Spain?

b10   *And which one was about husband-and-wife publishers (with Penelope Keith as the wife)?*

a11   *The Larkins* was originally a 1959 comedy series about Alf and Ada Larkin. Who played big-voiced Ada?

b11   *And who played Alf?*

a12   In which comedy were there characters called 'Cheese and Egg', 'Heavy Breathing' and 'Bloody Delilah'?

b12   *What was the 'situation' in the sitcom called* In Loving Memory?

No. 103 Answers

a1 Terry Scott and June Whitfield
b1 Terry and June
a2 *Are You Being Served?*
b2 *Nicholas Parsons*
a3 David Jason
b3 *Just Good Friends*
a4 *Dear John*
b4 Waiting for God
a5 The Two Ronnies (Ronnies Corbett and Barker)
b5 *(Gareth) Hale and (Norman) Pace*
a6 *Not in Front of the Children*
b6 All Gas and Gaiters
a7 *Till Death Us Do Part*
b7 *Chislebury Boys School*
a8 *The Army Game*
b8 Bootsie and Snudge *('Excused Boots' Bisley and Sgt Major Snudge)*
a9 Norman Beaton
b9 *Lenny Henry*
a10 *Duty Free*
b10 Executive Stress
a11 Peggy Mount
b11 *David Kossof*
a12 *The Dustbinmen*
b12 *It was set in an undertaker's (in Lancashire, in the Twenties)*

Tie-breaker

Q What was the name of the Steptoes' horse?
A *Hercules*

218

No. 104 Follow that Plot–2

Two of Shakespeare's best-known plays are *Julius Caesar* and *The Merchant of Venice*–but can you fill the gaps in these summaries of what happens in part of each play?

Team A
Julius Caesar, Act III, scene i
Caesar arrives at the Capitol attended by the senators and many others. Caesar refuses to read any petitions which concern himself. ...1... is led away by Trebonius. The conspirators then ...2... Caesar and he dies. Brutus and the other conspirators bathe their hands in ...3... and prepare to march to the market-place proclaiming that they have won peace, freedom and liberty for ...4... A servant arrives asking if ...1... may approach. Cassius still has fears about ...1... ...1... arrives and kneels over the body of Caesar. ...5... tries to explain why they felt they had to murder Caesar. ...1... shakes hands with each of them and asks permission to speak in Caesar's honour in the market-place. Despite a warning from ...6..., ...5... gives permission.

Team B
The Merchant of Venice, Act III, scenes iii and iv
In Venice, Antonio is under arrest. Shylock is angry that even under guard, Antonio should be allowed exercise in the street. Shylock repeats that he has no intention of renouncing the bond. Antonio has little hope that he will be spared, but prays that he may see his friend ...1... once more before he dies. At Belmont Portia and ...1..., and Nerissa and ...2... have been married, and the two men have set off for Venice to pay Shylock his money. Portia leaves ...3... and Jessica in command of her house and says that she and Nerissa will go to a nunnery until their husbands return. In fact, with the help of her cousin, Doctor ...4..., who is a lawyer, Portia is planning to go to Venice, disguised as a young ...5..., in order to try to save Antonio. Nerissa will go disguised as a ...6...

No. 104 Answers

Team A
1 Antony
2 stab (accept: kill, murder, assassinate)
3 Caesar's blood
4 Rome (accept: the people of Rome)
5 Brutus
6 Cassius

Team B
1 Bassanio
2 Gratiano
3 Lorenzo
4 Bellario
5 lawyer
6 lawyer's clerk

Tie-breaker

Q In which two Shakespeare plays are there characters called Moth?

A A Midsummer Night's Dream *(one of Titania's fairy attendants)* and Love's Labour's Lost *(Don Armado's page)*

No. 105 International Theatre

In this international round, teams could win more points the fewer clues they need to identify each director and each form of theatre. And, as a further clue, each answer begins with the letter 'K'!

Team A Director
1 This director is noted for the high intensity of his.
2 He was acclaimed for his stage productions of *On the Waterfront* and *East of Eden*.
3 In rehearsal, he would often take actors aside, his arm draped round their shoulders, and give a note privately.
4 He was the co-founder of the Actors' Studio and a proponent of the Method School of Acting.

Team B Director
1 A director and scenic designer, he started an underground theatre when the Nazis were in power.
2 He often appeared as a 'master of ceremonies' in his own plays.
3 In one of his most famous productions, his actors spent much of the time sitting at old school desks.
4 His company was called Cricot II and was based in Cracow in Poland.

Team A Theatre
1 Though the roots of this form of theatre go back to the year 1600, it is always up to date.
2 A characteristic of this style of theatre is for actors to freeze in tableaux at key dramatic moments.
3 Female roles are always played by men who specialize in female impersonation.

Team B Theatre
1 This theatrical form emerged in the seventeenth century.
2 It involves ritual, elaborate facial and eye expressions and 600 different hand gestures.
3 It is a blend of acting and dance and involves dramatizations from the Ramayana and Mahabharata.

No. 105 Answers

Team A Director
Elia Kazan (1909–)
His first major directional credit on film was *A Tree Grows in Brooklyn* (1945). His best work came in the 1950s when he worked with many of the actors at the forefront of the Method school of performing. Marlon Brando starred in his *On the Waterfront* (1954) and James Dean starred in *East of Eden* (1955).

Team B Director
Tadeusz Kantor (1915–1990)
He was a Polish scene designer and director. During the Nazi occupation of Poland he founded an underground independent theatre. In Cracow he organized his own theatre in 1956, calling it Cricot II. In the 1970s he developed 'The Theatre of Death', where time and death held sway, and Kantor himself appeared as a master of ceremonies. The play mentioned in clue 3 was *The Dead Class*.

Team A Theatre
Kabuki
This form of Japanese theatre began around 1600. *Kabuki* means unorthodox or new. Because Kabuki depends on a popular audience, it is always up to date, adapting its plays, music, dance and acting to the times. Actors of female roles develop a highly stylized form of acting in which the strength of a man and the delicacy of a woman are fused.

Team B Theatre
Kathakali
This form of dance drama comes from Southern India. It is a blend of dance, music and acting which dramatizes the Indian epics–Ramayana, Mahabharata and the Puranas. Originally, the sons of actors were trained in the art by their fathers. The ideas of a play are conveyed almost entirely through hand gestures and facial and body expressions. Meanwhile, the text of the play is chanted by two singers.

No. 106 Music Maestro, Please

Who either won or did well in the Eurovision Song Contest with...
a1   ...'Puppet on a String'?
b1   ...'Boom Bang-a-Bang'?
a2   ...'All Kinds of Everything'?
b2   ...'Waterloo'?
a3   ...'Making Your Mind Up'?
b3   ...'Jack in a Box'?

Which entertainers had successes with these comedy songs...
a4   ...'The Biggest Aspidistra in the World'?
b4   ...'Mr Wu's a Window Cleaner Now'?
a5   ...'I've Got a Lovely Bunch of Coconuts'?
b5   ...'Gilly, Gilly, Oscenfeffer, Katzenellen Bogen by the Sea'?
a6   ...'Mad Dogs and Englishmen'?
b6   ...'The Welly Boot Song'?

With which instrument do you associate...
a7   ...Larry Adler?
b7   ...Winifred Atwell?
a8   ...Eddie Calvert?
b8   ...Acker Bilk?
a9   ...John Dankworth?
b9   ...Max Jaffa?

By what name were these siblings better known...
a10   ...Jackie, Tito, Marlon, Jermaine and Michael?
b10   ...Alan, Wayne, Merril, Jay, Donny and Marie?
a11   ...LaVerne, Maxene and Patti?
b11   ...Richard and Karen?
a12   ...Don and Phil?
b12   ...Ruth, Anita, Bonnie and June?

No. 106 Answers

a1 Sandie Shaw
b1 Lulu
a2 Dana
b2 ABBA
a3 Bucks Fizz
b3 Clodagh Rogers
a4 Gracie Fields
b4 George Formby
a5 Billy Cotton (and his Band)
b5 Max Bygraves
a6 Noël Coward
b6 Billy Connolly
a7 Mouth organ (accept: harmonica)
b7 Piano
a8 Trumpet
b8 Clarinet
a9 Alto sax (accept: saxophone)
b9 Violin
a10 The Jacksons (The Jackson Five)
b10 The Osmonds
a11 The Andrews Sisters
b11 The Carpenters
a12 The Everly Brothers
b12 The Pointer Sisters

Tie-breaker

Q Which sensational black American artiste appeared at the *Folies Bergère* in Paris between the Wars and was famous for a jungle dance in which she wore only bananas?

A *Josephine Baker*

No. 107 Songs from the Shows–3

In which musical does each of the following numbers occur:

a1 'The Rain in Spain'?
b1 *'Food, Glorious Food'?*
a2 'Getting to Know You'?
b2 *'Sweet Transvestite'?*
a3 'Everything's Coming Up Roses'?
b3 *'The American Dream'?*
a4 'Prepare Ye the Way of the Lord'?
b4 *'I Don't Know How to Love Him'?*
a5 'We're Looking for a Piano'?
b5 *'Another Suitcase in Another Hall'?*
a6 'I Could Write a Book'?
b6 *'Baubles, Bangles and Beads'?*
a7 'I Hope I Get It'?
b7 *'You're the Top'?*
a8 'The Sun Has Got His Hat On'?
b8 *'Don't Rain on My Parade'?*
a9 'We'll Gather Lilacs'?
b9 *'Falling in Love With Love'?*
a10 'Anything But Lonely'?
b10 *'Shakin' at the High School Hop'?*
a11 'When Mabel Comes in the Room'?
b11 *'When Velma Takes the Stand'?*
a12 'There's a Small Hotel' and 'Slaughter on Tenth Avenue'?
b12 *'The Lady Is a Tramp' and 'My Funny Valentine'?*

No. 107 Answers

a1 *My Fair Lady*
b1 Oliver!
a2 *The King and I*
b2 The Rocky Horror Show
a3 *Gypsy*
b3 Miss Saigon
a4 *Godspell*
b4 Jesus Christ Superstar
a5 *Salad Days*
b5 Evita
a6 *Pal Joey*
b6 Kismet
a7 *A Chorus Line*
b7 Anything Goes
a8 *Me and My Girl*
b8 Funny Girl
a9 *Perchance to Dream*
b9 The Boys from Syracuse
a10 *Aspects of Love*
b10 Grease
a11 *Mack and Mabel*
b11 Chicago
a12 *On Your Toes*
b12 Babes in Arms

Tie-breaker

Q From which musical play come the numbers 'The Latin American Way', 'Sunnyside Lane' and 'S.A.D.U.S.E.A.'?

A Privates on Parade (S.A.D.U.S.E.A. is 'Song and Dance Unit, South East Asia)

No. 108 Classic Drama...

...on the small screen.

a1   In which series was everything 'Perfick...just perfick'?

b1   *Who played its male lead?*

a2   And who played his wife?

b2   *On whose novels was it based?*

In *Upstairs Downstairs*...

a3   ...what was the name of the butler?

b3   *...and what was the name of the cook?*

a4   ...who played the butler?

b4   *...and who played the cook?*

a5   In *Edward VII*, who played Edward?

b5   *Who played Queen Victoria?*

a6   In *The Six Wives of Henry VIII*, who played Henry?

b6   *Which BBC period serial starred Gemma Jones and was set in the Bentinck Hotel?*

a7   Which drama serial was about the Tyneside Seaton family during the Depression?

b7   *Who played the detective Albert Campion in* Campion?

a8   In the drama serial *Edward and Mrs Simpson*, who played Edward VIII?

b8   *And about whom was another 'costume' serial,* Lillie?

a9   In *The Forsyte Saga*, who played Fleur?

b9   *And who played Irene?*

a10   In which university was *Porterhouse Blue* set?

b10   *Who played the college porter, Skullion?*

a11   Which drama series about occupied Europe was set in a Belgium café?

b11   *Who played the café proprietor?*

a12   In the 1977 television production *Jesus of Nazareth*, who played Jesus?

b12   *And which famous cinema director made the two-part epic?*

No. 108 Answers

a1   *Darling Buds of May*
b1   *David Jason*
a2   Pam Ferris
b2   *H. E. Bates*
a3   Hudson
b3   *Mrs Bridges*
a4   Gordon Jackson
b4   *Angela Baddeley*
a5   Timothy West
b5   *Annette Crosbie*
a6   Keith Michell
b6   *Duchess of Duke Street*
a7   *When the Boat Comes In*
b7   *Peter Davison*
a8   Edward Fox
b8   *Lillie Langtry (a singer from Jersey who became Edward VII's mistress)*
a9   Susan Hampshire
b9   *Nyree Dawn Porter*
a10 Cambridge
b10 *David Jason*
a11 *Secret Army*
b11 *Bernard Hepton*
a12 Robert Powell
b12 *Franco Zeffirelli*

Tie-breaker

Q   Who wrote the novels which formed the basis of the costume drama serial *The Pallisers*?

A   *Anthony Trollope*

No. 109 Ciné Talk

What is...

a1 ...a dissolve?

b1 ...a cutaway?

a2 ...a print?

b2 ...a boom?

a3 ...ambient light?

b3 ...tracking?

a4 ...'stock shot' (or a 'library shot')?

b4 ...a second-unit?

a5 Who would 'lace' a film?

b5 Which word is now usually used to describe a cinema with several smallish auditoria?

a6 What are 'rushes'?

b6 What is a 'Steenbeck'?

a7 What is a 'whip pan'?

b7 What is meant if a cameraman is said to be 'zoom happy'?

a8 What is a blimp?

b8 What was a Nickelodeon?

a9 What is the BFI?

b9 What is BAFTA?

a10 What is cinema vérité?

b10 What is a 'film noir'?

Tie-breaker

Q What is the major difference between cinemascope and cinerama?

A *Cinemascope employs an extra wide screen; cinerama uses three adjacent cameras and three projectors to present the resulting images on a curved screen (to give a continuous picture)*

No. 109 Answers

a1   When one film image fades into another (so that we see both for a brief moment)

b1   *An extra shot, taken from another angle (to help during editing)*

a2   Film stock that has been exposed and developed

b2   *A fishing-rod type of device from which can be hung a microphone*

a3   Light occurring on location out of the control of the crew (e.g. the sun)

b3   *When the camera moves to follow the action*

a4   A scene or shot taken from a film that already exists

b4   *A small unit of technicians trusted to shoot location shots, action or crowd scenes not involving the director or principal actors*

a5   The projectionist ('lacing' it through the projector)

b5   *A multiplex*

a6   Prints of a day's filming 'rushed' back to the studio or location for viewing within a few hours (or overnight)

b6   *(German-made) film editing machine*

a7   When a camera turns sideways very quickly

b7   *He's using a zoom effect too often (closing in on a detail of a scene and/or pulling out to show a wider view)*

a8   A soundproof cover that fits over a camera while filming to absorb the noise of the camera

b8   *The earliest form of cinema (the admission price being one nickel)*

a9   British Film Institute (it supports all aspects of film culture: e.g. preservation, archiving, publishing)

b9   *British Academy of Film and Television Arts (open to 'senior creative workers' in both industries)*

a10   Feature films that have the qualities of documentary films; films that have a documentary-like realism

b10   *Usually, a film of the late Forties or early Fifties expressing some aspect of the gloom then widely felt (accept: a bleak or pessimistic film)*

No. 110 A Life Between Boards

With touching modesty, many actors who write their autobiographies call them simply something like *Walter Plinge–A Life*. (See the tie-breaker question on the next page.) However, many other stars do find more original titles for their life stories. So whose biographies or autobiographies are the following?

a1   *Thank Heaven for Little Girls?*
b1   *Dear Me?*
a2   *A Bright Particular Star?*
b2   *Loitering With Intent?*
a3   *Out On a Limb* and *Dance While You Can?*
b3   *Don't Laugh At Me?*
a4   *A Postillion Struck By Lightning?*
b4   *Prick Up Your Ears?*
a5   *Little Boy Lost* or *Rebel Without a Cause?*
b5   *Scene and Hird?*
a6   *An Actor and His Time?*
b6   *Fatal Charm?*
a7   *A Better Class of Person* and *Almost a Gentleman?*
b7   *What's It All About??*
a8   *The Moon's a Balloon?*
b8   *The Joker's Wild?*
a9   *So Much Love?*
b9   *The Dynamite Kid?*
a10 *Being an Actor?*
b10 Adolf Hitler: My Part in His Downfall *and* Goodbye, Soldier*?*

No. 110 Answers

a1 Maurice Chevalier (by Edward Behr)
b1 *Peter Ustinov*
a2 Maggie Smith (by Michael Coveney)
b2 *Peter O'Toole*
a3 Shirley MacLaine
b3 *Norman Wisdom*
a4 Dirk Bogarde
b4 *Joe Orton (by John Lahr)*
a5 James Dean (by Joe Hyams)
b5 *Thora Hird*
a6 John Gielgud
b6 *Rex Harrison (by·Alexander Walker)*
a7 John Osborne
b7 *Michael Caine*
a8 David Niven
b8 *Jack Nicholson (by John Parker)*
a9 Beryl Reid
b9 *Brian Blessed*
a10 Simon Callow
b10 *Spike Milligan*

Tie-breaker

Q Who was or is Walter Plinge?
A *A fictitious name sometimes printed in a Cast List when, for some reason, it is undesirable to give the real name of the actor playing a part*

No. 111 Hall of Fame

a1 'Can't act, can't sing, can dance a little' was said about whom?

b1 *Who played a private eye in* The Maltese Falcon *and the psychopathic captain in* The Caine Mutiny?

a2 Which actress and singer was in *Pillow Talk, Calamity Jane* and *Young at Heart?*

b2 *Which actress was married to Mickey Rooney, Artie Shaw and Frank Sinatra?*

a3 Which veteran American comedian played God in the film *Oh, God?*

b3 *Which female star sang the title song in* The Way We Were?

a4 Whose credits include *Von Ryan's Express, The Third Man* and *Brief Encounter?*

b4 *And whose credits include* Separate Tables, The Guns of Navarone *and* Casino Royale?

a5 Who became famous for creating routines involving patterns of rotating chorus girls?

b5 *Who played Bottom in* A Midsummer Night's Dream *and won an Oscar nomination for* Love Me or Leave Me?

a6 Which actress (billed as 'Little Mary') appeared in silent films including *Rebecca of Sunnybrook Farm, Pollyanna* and *Little Lord Fauntleroy?*

b6 *Who partnered Bob Hope in* Sorrowful Jones *and* Fancy Pants–*and then achieved television success with* I Love...?

a7 Which actor said of the character he was playing in *Little Caesar*, 'Mother of mercy, is this the end of Rico?'?

b7 *Who said, 'Anyone who hates small dogs and children can't be all bad'?*

a8 Who made her début in the 1939 film *Goodbye Mr Chips* and was also in *Random Harvest* and *The Happiest Millionaire?*

b8 *Which pin-up of the silent films played herself in* Airport '75?

a9 Who was the swashbuckling star of *Captain Blood* (1935) and *The Adventures of Robin Hood* (1938)?

b9 *Who was the equally swashbuckling hero of* The Three Musketeers *(1921) and* Robin Hood *(1922)?*

No. 111 Answers

a1 Fred Astaire
b1 *Humphrey Bogart*
a2 Doris Day
b2 *Ava Gardner*
a3 George Burns
b3 *Barbra Streisand*
a4 Trevor Howard
b4 *David Niven*
a5 Busby Berkeley
b5 *James Cagney*
a6 Mary Pickford
b6 *Lucille Ball (I Love Lucy)*
a7 Edward G. Robinson
b7 *W. C. Fields*
a8 Greer Garson
b8 *Gloria Swanson*
a9 Errol Flynn
b9 *Douglas Fairbanks (Senior)*

Tie-breaker

Q Which French actor played opposite Greta Garbo in *Conquest* (1937)?

A *Charles Boyer*

No. 112 Hidden Titles–12

Within each of these dialogues are hidden the titles of eight classic farces. Can you spot the titles and say who wrote each play?

Team A

He (*Approaching*) Where are you dear? Ah, can you a spare a second?

She Not now darling, I'm cooking. Dinner.

He Mm. Gorgeous. Can I help?

She Just make the tea. I'm doing the sauce for the goose.

He Lovely. Tea. Two spoons–and one for the pot. Milk?

She And honey. Now what did you want?

He Does...this suit me?

She A boater?

He Actually it's Italian.

She An Italian straw hat! That should put the cat among the pigeons at the cricket club.

He Why on earth should it–

She You'll be like a cuckoo in the nest. They'll just chuck you out and you'll run for your wife.

Team B

He (*Imitating front door bell*) Boying-boying!

She (*Refined*) What's that?

He Listen!

She What?

He (*With a slight lisp*) (T)hark! I thought I heard the front door bell.

She If they're selling anything, don't commit yourself. We can't afford it. Anyway, only fools rush in and sign straight away.

He If I don't want to buy anything, you'll see how they run away.

She It wasn't like that with that man offering to get the cellar dry.

He Rot! I didn't sign in the end.

She It was a close shave.

He (*Going to the door*) I'll tell them to come back on Monday next.

She (*Calling*) And if it's the man for the rent, you'll just have to say we can't pay. (*To herself*) Won't pay, more like.

No. 112 Answers

Team A titles
Not Now Darling by Ray Cooney and John Chapman
Sauce for the Goose by Georges Feydeau
One for the Pot by Ray Cooney
Milk and Honey by Philip King
An Italian Straw Hat by Eugène Labiche
Cat Among the Pigeons by Georges Feydeau
A Cuckoo in the Nest by Ben Travers
Run for Your Wife by Ray Cooney

Team B titles
Boeing-Boeing by Marc Camoletti & Beverley Cross
Thark by Ben Travers
Fools Rush In by Kenneth Horne
See How They Run by Philip King
Dry Rot by John Chapman
A Close Shave by Georges Feydeau
On Monday Next by Philip King
Can't Pay, Won't Pay by Dario Fo

No. 113 Television Meets Real Life

On what subject were (or are) the following 'telly pundits'...
a1   ...Percy Thrower?
b1   ...David Bellamy?
a2   ...A. J. P. Taylor?
b2   ...Mortimer Wheeler?
a3   Who were Jasmine Bligh and Elizabeth Cowell?
b3   And what role in television was shared by Christopher Chataway and Robin Day?
a4   Who presented the documentary series America?
b4   And who presented The Body in Question series?
a5   What used to be the subtitle of BBC TV's Panorama?
b5   On 1st April, 1957, Panorama carried a 'joke' report about the harvest of which crop?
a6   Which television personality cried when he was interviewed on television's Face to Face?
b6   Which novelist spoke very frankly on the same programme?
a7   What was the purpose of the programme On the Move?
b7   Who presented ITV's motoring magazine Drive-In?
a8   Which documentary investigated killings in Gibraltar?
b8   Which television company made the programme?
a9   About which war was the film Tumbledown?
b9   Which country took offence at the drama documentary Death of a Princess?
a10   Who was reading the BBC News when the studio was invaded by lesbians?
b10   Who was discomfited by Mrs Gould on Nationwide?
a11   Which television journalist was held captive in Beirut for five years?
b11   Which show ended tragically when a member of the public was killed in a stunt?
a12   Which 'royal' took part in a TV quiz in 1987?
b12   In which show did four royals captain teams?

No. 113 Answers

a1 Gardening

b1 *Botany or ecology*

a2 History

b2 *Archaeology*

a3 Pre-war television announcers (Jasmine Bligh also introduced programmes when BBC Television resumed in 1946)

b3 *They were among ITN's first newscasters*

a4 Alistair Cooke

b4 *Jonathan Miller*

a5 'The Window on the World'

b5 *Spaghetti*

a6 Gilbert Harding

b6 *Evelyn Waugh*

a7 To teach adults to read; to improve adult literacy

b7 *Shaw Taylor*

a8 *Death On the Rock*

b8 *Thames Television*

a9 Falklands War

b9 *Saudi Arabia*

a10 Sue Lawley (she carried on reading while Nicholas Witchell battled out of vision)

b10 *Mrs Thatcher (Mrs Gould, a member of the public, questioned the then Prime Minister about the sinking of the Belgrano during the Falklands conflict)*

a11 John McCarthy

b11 The Late, Late Breakfast Show

a12 Princess Anne

b12 The Grand Knockout Tournament *(accept:* It's a Knockout*)*

Tie-breaker

Q Who was the first woman to read the national news on BBC TV?

A *Nan Winton (in 1960)*

No. 114 Wireless World

Which DJ is associated with the catch phrase...
a1 ...'Greetings, pop-pickers'?
b1 ..."Ello, darlin'!'?
a2 ...'As it 'appens'?
b2 ...'What's the recipe today, Jim?'?

From which town or city do these commercial radio stations broadcast...
a3 ...Radio Broadland?
b3 ...Hallam FM?
a4 ...Piccadilly?
b4 ...Red Dragon?
a5 ...Downtown Radio?
b5 ...BRMB?

In which radio show do or did we hear...
a6 ...the Tuckers, Tregorrans and Grundys?
b6 ...Bob, Gwen and Mrs Maggs?
a7 ...Denis Bloodnok, Henry Crun and Neddy?
b7 ...Jimmy, Susan and Grandad?
a8 ...Mona Lott, Sophie Tuckbox and Ali Oop?
b8 ...Ben, Bebe and Aggie?
a9 ...Sarah, Eleanor, Clare and Russell?
b9 ...Alex, Anita Sharma, Hugh and the Brennans?

Who wrote...
a10 ...Take It from Here?
b10 ...Hancock's Half Hour?
a11 ...The Hitchhiker's Guide to the Galaxy?
b11 ...ITMA?
a12 ...Journey Into Space?
b12 ...Dick Barton–Special Agent! and the early Archers scripts?

No. 114 Answers

a1 Alan Freeman
b1 *Ed Stewart*
a2 Jimmy Savile
b2 *Jimmy Young*
a3 Norwich
b3 *Sheffield*
a4 Manchester
b4 *Cardiff (and Newport)*
a5 Belfast
b5 *Birmingham*
a6 *The Archers*
b6 *Mrs Dale's Diary* (later, *The Dales*)
a7 *The Goon Show*
b7 The Clitheroe Kid
a8 *ITMA* (*It's That Man Again*)
b8 Life With the Lyons
a9 *After Henry*
b9 Citizens
a10 Frank Muir and Denis Norden
b10 *Ray Galton and Alan Simpson*
a11 Douglas Adams
b11 *Ted Kavanagh*
a12 Charles Chilton
b12 *Edward J. Mason* (Dick Barton *with Geoffrey Webb*)

Tie-breaker

Q Which was the first legal independent local radio station to broadcast in England?

A *LBC (London Broadcasting Company)*

No. 115 Prompt, Please

A round of famous lines from well-known plays and films—but, in each case, what line comes next?

a1 'My goodness, those diamonds are lovely.'
b1 *'I've got to take under my wing, tra-la...'*
a2 'The Book of Life begins with a man and a woman in a garden.'
b2 *'The last temptation is the greatest treason...'*
a3 'Ill-met by moonlight, proud Titania.'
b3 *'Are you going to walk across the park, Miss Doolittle?'*
a4 'Let's go.'
'We can't.'
'Why not?'
b4 *'When constabulary's duty to be done...'*
a5 'I may smoke one pipe of asthma mixture...'
b5 *'The sixth age shifts*
Into the lean and slipper'd pantaloon...'
a6 'When I see a spade, I call it a spade.'
b6 *'Tis brief my Lord...'*
a7 'For you dream you are crossing the Channel and tossing about in a steamer from Harwich...'
b7 *'For God's sake, let us sit upon the ground...'*
a8 'I said to this monk, here I said, you haven't got a pair of shoes, have you, a pair of shoes, I said, enough to keep me on my way.'
b8 *And lastly, which play title comes from the song whose chorus begins:*
'Bless 'em all, bless 'em all.'

Tie-breaker

Q What follows this line from Shakespeare's *Hamlet*?:
'There are more things in heaven and earth, Horatio...
A *...than are dreamt of in your philosophy.'*

No. 115 Answers

a1   'Goodness had nothing to do with it, dearie.'–Mae West in the
         film *Night After Night*

b1   *'A most unattractive old thing, tra-la*
         With a caricature of a face.'–The Mikado *by W. S. Gilbert*

a2   'It ends with revelations.'–Lord Illingworth and Mrs Allonby in
         A Woman of No Importance by Oscar Wilde

b2   *'To do the right deed for the wrong reason.'*–Becket *in* Murder in
         the Cathedral *by T. S. Eliot*

a3   'What, jealous Oberon!'–Oberon and Titania in Shakespeare's
         A Midsummer Night's Dream

b3   *'Walk! Not bloody likely. I am going in a Taxi.'*–Freddie and Eliza
         in Pygmalion *by G. B. Shaw (accept: 'Not bloody likely.')*

a4   'We're waiting for Godot.'–Estragon and Vladimir in Samuel
         Beckett's *Waiting for Godot*

b4   *'The policeman's lot is not a happy one.'*–Pirates of Penzance *by*
         W. S. Gilbert

a5   *'In the woodshed, if you please.'*–Mr Pritchard and Mrs Ogmore-
         Pritchard in Under Milk Wood *by Dylan Thomas*

b5   *'With spectacles on nose and pouch on side.'*–Jacques in
         Shakespeare's As You Like It

a6   'I am glad to say I have never seen a spade.'–Cecily and
         Gwendolen in *The Importance of Being Earnest* by Oscar Wilde

b6   *'As woman's love.'*–Ophelia and Hamlet in Shakespeare's Hamlet

a7   'Which is something between a large bathing machine and a very
         small second-class carriage.'–*Iolanthe* by W. S. Gilbert

b7   *'And tell sad stories of the death of kings.'*–The King in
         Shakespeare's Richard II

a8   'Piss off, he said.'–Davies, the tramp, in Harold Pinter's *The Caretaker*

b8   The Long and the Short and the Tall *by Willis Hall*

No. 116 Music Hall

In the days of music hall, which artiste was originally associated with the songs...

a1   ...'I Love a Lassie' and 'Roamin' in the Gloamin"?

b1   ...'Oh Mr Porter' and 'The Boy I Love Is Up in the Gallery'?

a2   ...'Down at the Old Bull and Bush' and 'Pack up all Your Troubles'?

b2   ...'Daddie Wouldn't Buy me a Bow-wow' and 'Waiting at the Church'?

a3   ...'Champagne Charlie'?

b3   ...'I'm Shy, Mary Ellen'?

a4   ...'All the Nice Girls Love a Sailor'?

b4   ...'My Old Dutch' and 'Knocked 'em in the Old Kent Road'?

Who was the star who...

a5   ...played a drunken Scotsman who sang 'I belong to Glasgow'?

b5   ...was nicknamed 'the Prime Minister of Mirth'?

a6   ...sang 'Boiled Beef and Carrots' and 'I'm Hen-e-ry the Eighth I Am'?

b6   ...was a pantomime dame, famous for his rubbery face–and was one of the greatest music hall personalities?

a7   ...was famous for her male impersonations, singing 'Burlington Bertie' and often appearing as a sailor or soldier?

b7   ...who sang 'I'm Burlington Bertie from Bow'?

And, between the Wars, which comedian...

a8   ...sang 'If It Wasn't for the 'Ouses in Between'?

b8   ...sang 'The Lily of Laguna'?

a9   ...played the banjolele, singing 'I kept my ukelele in my hand'?

b9   ...often played an inadequate schoolmaster in gown and mortar board, with glasses perched on the end of his nose?

a10 ...played a character called Mr Muddlecombe JP and was also famous for his war-time monologues?

b10 ...was 'almost a gentleman', invented the 'boom-boom' pay-off to a joke and was famous for his monologues?

No. 116 Answers

a1   Harry Lauder
b1   *Marie Lloyd (also: Nellie Power)*
a2   Florrie Forde
b2   *Vesta Victoria*
a3   George Leybourne
b3   *Jack Pleasants*
a4   Hetty King
b4   *Albert Chevalier*
a5   Will Fyffe
b5   *George Robey*
a6   Harry Champion
b6   *Dan Leno*
a7   Vesta Tilley
b7   *Ella Shields*
a8   Gus Elen
b8   *Eugene Stratton*
a9   George Formby
b9   *Will Hay*
a10 Robb Wilton
b10 *Billy Bennett*

Tie-breaker

Q Who was particularly associated with these songs: 'Hello, Hello, Who's Your Lady Friend?', 'Who Were You with Last Night?' and 'Here We Are, Here We Are Again'?

A *Mark Sheridan*

No. 117 I Never Read the Notices

A critic is said to be someone who leaves no turn unstoned (a saying attributed to various writers, including one Revd Joseph McCulloch)– and no actor is immune.

Can you deduce for which play each of these actors collected the following cruel notices?

a1 'Flora Robson accepts the news of her son's syphilis with an air of a district nurse facing an epidemic of sniffles.'

b1 *'Rather than play the part, Alastair Sim chooses to reconnoitre it. You might think him a tentative pantomime dame standing in for Tommy Cooper, the music hall magician whose tricks never work.' (And this was about a Shakespearian production!)*

a2 'Towards the end, when he is bowed and grey but unbroken, Mr Scofield comes into his own for greyness is then needed.' (Paul Scofield played this role on stage and on screen.)

b2 *'Matters are not helped by Mr Tommy Steele's attempt to make the party go by shouting the house down as Tony Lumpkin. Audiences later in the run will be spared the worst, as Mr Steele is headed for laryngitis within the week at this rate.'*

a3 '(He) is the finest actor on earth from the neck up.'

b3 *'I had another look at St Joan and saw you trying your pet stunts for all they were worth. They failed completely, as I told you they would.' (This remark was made by the author of the play.)*

a4 'She barged down the Nile last night as Cleopatra and sank.'

b4 *'As Charley's Aunt he reminded me of Whistler's mother.'*

Turning to television...

a5 When television's *Coronation Street* celebrated its 21st birthday, which poet sent this telegram:
'The Street grows richer and deeper and more lovable year by year. I thank God for it and live for Mondays and Wednesdays'?

b5 *And who sent this telegram from 'The Bull':*
'Congratulations on being able to drink legally in the Rover's Return...You'll be there in body as we will in spirit'?

No. 117 Answers

a1   Mrs Alving in *Ghosts* by Ibsen, reviewed by Alan Brien

b1   *Prospero in* The Tempest *reviewed by Kenneth Tynan*

a2   Sir Thomas More in *A Man For All Seasons* by Robert Bolt, reviewed by Bernard Levin

b2   *Tony Lumpkin in* She Stoops to Conquer *by Oliver Goldsmith, reviewed by Bernard Levin*

a3   Sir John Gielgud (Kenneth Tynan on Sir John's one man 'show' *The Ages of Man*. In 1924, Sir John was described by another critic, Ivor Brown, as having 'the most meaningless legs imaginable'.)

b3   *Wendy Hiller (Bernard Shaw, in a letter to Miss Hiller, about her role in his* St Joan*)*

a4   Tallulah Bankhead (in Shakespeare's *Antony and Cleopatra*, reviewed by James Mason Brown)

b4   *Tom Courtenay (Frank Marcus on Mr Courtenay's performance in* Charley's Aunt *by Brandon Thomas)*

a5   Sir John Betjeman

b5   *Radio's* Archer *family*

Tie-breaker

Q   Which critic defended his craft by saying: 'A critic is a man who knows the way but can't drive the car'?

A   *Kenneth Tynan*

No. 118 Telly Mixtures

First, a selection of questions about children's television:

On *The Muppet Show...*

a1 ...what was the name of the bear?

b1 *...and of Kermit's nephew?*

a2 ...who was the drummer?

b2 *...and what was the piano-playing dog called?*

a3 In which children's show was there a 'Double or Drop' quiz?

b3 *What booby prize were you given for a wrong answer?*

a4 What was the name of Fred and Wilma Flintstone's daughter?

b4 *Who adopted the orphan Bamm Bamm?*

a5 Who played 'Mr Pastry' in the Fifties?

b5 *Who 'operated' or partnered Lenny the Lion?*

a6 Who originally narrated the *Thomas the Tank Engine* series?

b6 *Who first hosted* The Multi-Coloured Swap Shop?

a7 Who created *Grange Hill*?

b7 *Which character (played by Todd Carty) later got his own series?*

And secondly—a few questions about television's history:

a8 From where did the first BBC Television programmes come?

b8 *From which city was* Pebble Mill At One *broadcast?*

a9 From which city was *The Good Old Days* broadcast?

b9 *Which television company created the* Survival *wildlife series?*

a10 What was the group name of the singers in *The Black and White Minstrel Show*?

b10 *What was the name of the dance troupe in the same show?*

a11 How did BBC Radio upstage commercial television on the night the latter started up?

b11 *Who were Hullabaloo and Custard?*

a12 In which year did ITV begin broadcasting?

b12 *And in which year did BBC-2 begin?*

No. 118 Answers

a1 Fozzie
b1 *Robin*
a2 Animal
b2 *Rowlf*
a3 *Crackerjack*
b3 *A cabbage*
a4 Pebbles
b4 *Barney and Betty Rubble (accept: The Rubbles)*
a5 Richard Hearne
b5 *Terry Hall*
a6 Ringo Starr (later Michael Angelis)
b6 *Noel Edmonds*
a7 Phil Redmond
b7 *Tucker Jenkins (in Tucker's Luck)*
a8 Alexandra Palace
b8 *Birmingham*
a9 Leeds
b9 *Anglia Television*
a10 The George Mitchell Singers
b10 *The Television Toppers*
a11 Grace Archer (in the serial *The Archers*) was 'killed' in a fire
b11 *The mother and baby kangaroos used to advertise the launch of BBC-2*
a12 1955
b12 *1964*

Tie-breaker

Q Which quiz show was the first programme shown on Channel 4?
A Countdown

No. 119 Around the World–1

Provide the name of the city, town, street or other place that completes the titles of these plays, films and musicals.

NB Instead of using this round for a quiz between two teams, it could be used as a test of one team: how many titles can you complete in 30 or 40 seconds? (See also Quiz No. 120)

a1   *The Two Gentlemen of...?*
b1   The Pirates of...?
a2   *The Boys from...?*
b2   An American in...?
a3   *The Barber of...?*
b3   The Thief of...?
a4   *West of...?*
b4   Lawrence of...?
a5   *The Barretts of...?*
b5   Flying Down to...?
a6   *Scott of the...?*
b6   A Funny Thing Happened on the Way to...?
a7   *Slaughter on...?*
b7   The Man of...?
a8   *It Came From...?*
b8   The Best Little Whorehouse in...?
a9   *East of...?*
b9   A Tree Grows in...?
a10   *A Kind of...?*
b10   55 Days in...?
a11   *Picnic at...?*
b11   Nightmare on...?
a12   *All Quiet on the...?*
b12   The Playboy of the...?

No. 119 Answers

a1 *Verona*
b1 Penzance
a2 *Syracuse* or *Brazil*
b2 Paris
a3 *Seville*
b3 Baghdad
a4 *Suez* or *Broadway* or *Shanghai* or *Zanzibar*
b4 Arabia
a5 *Wimpole Street*
b5 Rio
a6 *Antarctic*
b6 The Forum
a7 *Tenth Avenue*
b7 La Mancha
a8 *Outer Space*
b8 Texas
a9 *Eden* or *Piccadilly* or *Sudan*
b9 Brooklyn
a10 *Alaska*
b10 Peking
a11 *Hanging Rock*
b11 Elm Street
a12 *Western Front*
b12 Western World

Tie-breaker

Q Which film director said: 'The cinema is not a slice of life, it's a piece of cake'?

A *Alfred Hitchcock*

No. 120 Around the World–2

Provide the name of the city, town, street or other place that completes the titles of these plays, films and musicals.

NB Instead of using this round for a quiz between two teams, it could be used as a test of one team: how many titles can you complete in 30 or 40 seconds? (See also Quiz No. 119)

a1 *The Merchant of...?*
b1 A Passage to...?
a2 *April in...?*
b2 Timon of...?
a3 *Passport to...?*
b3 The Wizard of...?
a4 *The Jew of...?*
b4 Seagulls Over...?
a5 *Death in...?*
b5 The Last Days of...?
a6 *Ring Round the...?*
b6 Meet Me in...?
a7 *The Snows of...?*
b7 Last Tango in...?
a8 *The Good Woman of...?*
b8 Shut Your Eyes and Think of...?
a9 *84...?*
b9 Good Morning...?
a10 *A Chump at...?*
b10 The Count of...?
a11 *Breakfast at...?*
b11 Death on the...?
a12 *Gunfight at the...?*
b12 The Dame of...?

No. 120 Answers

a1   *Venice*
b1   India
a2   *Paris*
b2   Athens
a3   *Pimlico*
b3   Oz
a4   *Malta*
b4   Sorrento
a5   *Venice*
b5   Pompeii *or* Dolwyn
a6   *Moon*
b6   St Louis
a7   *Kilimanjaro*
b7   Paris
a8   *Szechuan*
b8   England
a9   *Charing Cross Road*
b9   Vietnam
a10   *Oxford*
b10   Monte Cristo
a11   *Tiffany's*
b11   Nile
a12   *OK Corral* (*NB* There are also films called *Gunfight at Comanche Creek* and *Gunfight at Dodge City*)
b12   Sark

Tie-breaker

Q Which movie mogul said: 'The cinema would be greatly improved if they shot less film and more producers'?
A *Sam Goldwyn*

No. 33 Answers

Team A

Shakespeare
Speech 1 comes from *Titus Andronicus*, Act II, scene ii. Titus is speaking to his three sons, out hunting with hounds, early one morning.

Speech 2 comes from *King John*, Act III, scene i. Constance, mother of the little prince Arthur (who is nephew of King John) is talking to her friend, the honest Earl of Salisbury.

Speech 3 is 'phoney'.

Team B

Chekhov
Speech 1 is spoken by Ivan Nyukhin in the monologue, *Smoking Is Bad For You*.

Speech 2 is spoken by Olga in *The Three Sisters*.

Speech 3 contains phrases from various plays but does not occur in any known Chekhov play!

No. 66 Answers

Team A

Ibsen
Speech 1 is Nora Helmer talking to her husband Torvald in Act III of
A Doll's House.

Speech 2 is Solness, the 'master builder' himself, talking to Hilde
Wangel, the young woman who hero-worships him (and encourages
him later to climb the spire from which he falls to his death)—in Act II of
The Master Builder.

Speech 3 does contain one or two phrases that have been 'stolen' from
The Wild Duck—but Mrs Alving is a character in *Ghosts*.

Team B

Wilde
Speech 1 is the Duchess of Berwick talking to Lady Windermere (about
Lord Windermere) in Act I of *Lady Windermere's Fan*.

Speech 2 is the impostor.

Speech 3 is Lord Goring talking to Sir Robert Chiltern in Act II of *An
Ideal Husband*.

No. 99 Answers

Team A
Speech 1 is not by Pinter.

Speech 2 is said by Mick in *The Caretaker*.

Speech 3 is said by the First Old Woman in the revue sketch *The Black and White*.

Team B
Speech 1 is not by Beckett.

Speech 2 is Hamm talking to Clov in *Endgame*.

Speech 3 is Pozzo talking to the two tramps, Estragon and Vladimir (in Act I) of *Waiting for Godot*.